D0873833

fP

Lipstick on a Pig

WINNING IN THE NO-SPIN ERA BY
SOMEONE WHO KNOWS THE GAME

Torie Clarke

FREE PRESS

New York   London   Toronto   Sydney

FREE PRESS
A Division of Simon & Schuster, Inc.
1230 Avenue of the Americas
New York, NY 10020

FREE PRESS and colophon are trademarks
of Simon & Schuster, Inc.

For information regarding special discounts for bulk purchases,
please contact Simon & Schuster Special Sales at
1-800-456-6798 or business@simonandschuster.com

Designed by Kyoko Watanabe

Manufactured in the United States of America

10   9   8   7   6   5   4   3   2

Library of Congress Cataloging-in-Publication
Data Control Number 2005054932

ISBN-13: 978-0-7432-7116-5
ISBN-10: 0-7432-7116-5

*To the men and women
of the Armed Forces of America,
because they have the best story to tell*

Public sentiment is everything. With public sentiment, nothing can fail; without it, nothing can succeed.

—ABRAHAM LINCOLN

CONTENTS

OPERATING INSTRUCTIONS

I wrote this book because several smart people for whom I have much respect said I should. I also wrote it because I believe deeply that people deserve to hear as much as possible from their corporate and public leaders. Maybe if those leaders read this book, I thought, they'll be more willing to assume the communications functions inherent in their leadership roles. And I wrote it because I realized that something I have done for years—connect with people—has taken on added importance in the information era. As geographical boundaries blur and interactions increase, the ability to communicate effectively has bottom-line impacts on governments and corporations around the world. Now more than ever, people need to know how to communicate.

I love to tell stories—as my friends and family patiently bear witness—so I thought the best way to write this book was to articulate broad principles and illuminate them with stories I find meaningful. Doing so chronologically would have been easier, but not as persuasive. So I apologize that some sections skip around in time and hope I've matched the right stories with the right principles.

A few warnings are in order. With the exception of scattered notes I took at the Pentagon on 9/11, I have never taken or saved notes at my many jobs and from which I drew most of the anecdotes in this book. I've done my best to recreate them accurately, using public record (e.g., articles and Department of Defense transcripts) whenever possible, and running many sections by the people involved to get their recollection of how events transpired.

I am sure some readers will want more detailed information about tools one can use to exploit the promise and avoid the perils of the Information Age. To me, many of them are more tactical—how to prepare for a big interview, for example, or how to develop key messages for a product or initiative rollout. Those are important skills and habits to have, to be sure, but not quite right for this book.

I am absolutely positive that in my career I have violated some of the principles I advocate. Heck, within the book itself, I probably violate a few. If I get wind of any egregious mistakes—both past and recent—I will try to correct them.

I hope *Lipstick on a Pig* helps people. Whether you are in business or government or academia, how you communicate what you're doing is as important as what you're actually doing.

Lipstick
on a Pig

CHAPTER 1

You Can Put a Lot of Lipstick on a Pig, but It's Still a Pig

---

*Deliver the bad news yourself,
and when you screw up, say so—fast!*

If you could only know one thing about Charles Keating—the man who came to personify the savings-and-loan crisis of the late eighties—the thing to know is that he never, not once that I ever saw, carried his own briefcase. Keating had an entourage for earthly tasks, a gaggle of high-powered lobbyists who trailed him in cowed silence wherever he went. Three hundred and sixty-four days of the year, they strutted around D.C. like peacocks in $1,800 suits. The one day Keating was in town they had to carry his briefcase. It was, depending on your perspective, pathetic, poetic justice, or both.

The entourage was always a spectacle to behold, never more so than one early afternoon in March 1987, when I was working as Senator John McCain's press secretary. Keating and his crew blew by my office, exuding indignant rage.

For weeks, Keating had harangued his contacts in the Senate, of which McCain was one, to get federal regulators who were looking into Keathing's company, Lincoln Savings & Loan, off his back. Keating was a political supporter and a personal friend of the family as well. The request put McCain in a tough spot: Keating was also Arizona's largest employer; it was reasonable for a senator to look into the matter on behalf of his constituents. Moreover, McCain felt that after months of investigation, the regulators needed to make a decision about Lincoln one way or the other. They should either crack down or move on and let everybody go about their business.

Keating, though, wasn't one to be satisfied with restrained inquiry. By the time he barged into McCain's office that spring day in 1987, he had a list of demands for the senator. That was his first mistake. McCain's a fair guy; he'll listen to requests, he encourages open discussion, but he's not the type to whom you put ultimatums. Keating's second screwup—the big one—was calling McCain a coward for failing to step and fetch when presented with the list. A few angry words later—McCain doesn't need many of them to get his point across—Keating was on his way out the door. At the time, all it seemed to be was a brief flash of twisted entertainment for a bored staff on an otherwise slow day.

The slow days wouldn't last for long.

In the months that followed, McCain and four other senators participated in two meetings with regulators. Some of the senators pled Keating's case aggressively. McCain's intervention, if it can be called that, was delicate: He said explicitly that he was inquiring only on a constituent's behalf. The regulators should do their jobs; he wanted to gather information, not apply pressure. But they did feel pressure. They would say later that the fact of the meeting itself—even if McCain and the other senators said nothing at all—conveyed an unspoken message: get off Keating's back.

Within two years, Lincoln Savings & Loan collapsed under a $2 billion mudslide of stupidity and corruption. Stories about the senators' meetings began to hit the headlines. The Keating Five scandal was under way.

At first, McCain was flitting around the periphery of the story. The press seemed more interested in other senators who appeared to have done more on Keating's behalf. In the summer of 1989, though, the *Arizona Republic* started an investigation into McCain's ties to Keating.

McCain's instincts told him the story would be bigger than the rest of us guessed. In the fall of 1989, on the Saturday before the *Republic* story was supposed to appear, I was hosting a pig roast on the cramped patio of my apartment in D.C. McCain was supposed to stop by but never showed. By nightfall, Mark Salter, his then foreign policy legislative assistant, and I had put a few beers back. Mark was on the patio dousing the pig with lighter fluid in a vain attempt to get the thing to catch fire and cook. I was sitting on the kitchen counter when the phone rang. It was McCain. The normal exuberance was missing from his voice.

"I'm sorry I'm not there," he said. "I don't want to be a wet blanket."

"John," I laughed, "you couldn't be a wet blanket if you tried."

McCain had a bad feeling about the story, and the next morning's *Republic* proved his instincts right. A detailed account of McCain's relationship with Keating—campaign contributions, personal friendship, joint family vacations at Keating's place in the Bahamas—was splashed across page one. McCain instantly moved to the forefront of the scandal.

McCain's advisers were split on how to handle the story. The other four senators were, for the most part, trying to lie low. The conventional wisdom for a story like this was to get on with your business and not talk about it. I disagreed. This story was too big. All the ingredients were there: taxpayers who had been ripped off, politicians who appeared corrupt. The press wasn't going to let go. Leaving the charges unanswered would make them look true. What was more, I felt we had a good, fair, accurate story to tell: As he would say, McCain shouldn't have gone to the meetings in the first place. But he had been careful not to pressure the regulators, and the moment he heard Keating was being accused of criminal activity, he backed off entirely. Other aides—the lawyers especially—insisted that McCain stay silent. That, too, was conventional wisdom: an investigation was under way, they said, and a potential subject of it should just keep his mouth shut.

McCain thought it over and called a staff meeting.

"Here's what we gotta do," he said, sitting behind a massive, ornate desk that belonged to McCain's mentor and predecessor, Barry Goldwater. "I want to have a press conference in Arizona. I will answer every question anyone wants to ask.

We'll stay as long as we need to. When we get back, I'm going to take every press call on this thing that comes in. I don't care where they're from or who they report for. And I want all of you to remember that we're going to have to work twice as hard on our normal legislative duties to show the people back home that we aren't being distracted by this."

My only concern about the press conference was McCain's temper. He's a laid-back guy, a jokester most of the time, but he's capable of blowing his top, especially when his honor is questioned. I cautioned McCain on it.

"OK," he said, "I'll tell you what. You sit in the front row, and any time you think I'm overdoing it, rub your nose with your forefinger."

A sophisticated clandestine operation it wasn't, but it worked. We booked a bare, low-ceilinged meeting room in a Phoenix hotel. As McCain walked to the podium, a crowd of dozens of reporters from around the country overflowed the room. McCain's opening statement was short and direct. Our intention was to take a tough issue and air it out. A long, lawyerly explanation would have looked like an attempt to cloud the issue. McCain just gave a brief account of his meetings with the regulators and said he would stay at the press conference as long as it took to answer every question. He did: it took about an hour and a half, and while the questions were tough, they were mostly fair. And I never had to rub my nose.

When we got back to Washington, McCain repeated his instructions to me. "We're going to take every last press call," he said. And he did. We spent months categorizing press calls by a sort of journalistic triage. Reporters on a tight deadline talked to McCain first. In cases of a time conflict, an Arizona journalist got the call before a national reporter. Depending on what time zone he was in, McCain started returning press calls as early as six a.m. and often didn't finish until well after dark.

It was tough going, but the strategy worked. By diving straight in and doing it early, McCain was able to get his message out before the story took over and got out of control. His candor earned reporters' respect. And perhaps most important, the fact that he was talking at all communicated something important to his constituents: McCain didn't have anything to hide.

"This man is a United States senator," said Roger Mudd, introducing a segment on the *MacNeil/Lehrer NewsHour* in November 1989. "He is John McCain, a Republican from Arizona, and you are about to hear him say something that very few senators have ever said before. Listen carefully."

"It was a very serious mistake on my part. The appearance of a meeting with five senators was bad and wrong and I agonized over it at the time." It was a clip from McCain's Arizona press conference.

"The four other senators involved in the Keating story, Democrats Cranston of California, DeConcini of Arizona, Glenn of Ohio, and Riegle of Michigan, all had been following a policy of stonewalling the press," Mudd said on the show. "McCain, however, seems to be trying to talk the story to death."

"I'm doing everything I can to try and set the record straight, again, admitting that I made mistakes, and serious ones," McCain said in one of the clips Mudd showed of the senator granting numerous interviews. "But I did not abuse my office, and I think that's the key to this issue. The fact is, I want to talk to anybody that wants to talk to me because I feel the more that is known of my involvement in this issue, the better off I am."

In that *MacNeil/Lehrer NewsHour,* Mudd called McCain's "open-door policy" a roll of the dice. McCain plays a mean game of craps, so he knows something about rolling dice. His strategy paid off. The Senate Ethics Committee outside counsel, Robert Bennett (a Democrat), largely absolved McCain; he survived the scandal and went on to forge a very successful Senate career and a strong presidential run in the 2000 Republican primaries.

Lessons from the Keating Five scandal served me well during a dustup at the Pentagon. That crisis—every day, it seemed, had at least one—involved Lieutenant General Michael W. Hagee. Hagee—a brainiac, a Marine's Marine, revered by uniforms and civilians alike—was about to reach the high point of his career: taking the oath as the thirty-third commandant of the Marine Corps.

Hagee's ascension, while important, wasn't on my radar screen. He sailed through Senate confirmation. His swearing-in ceremony was only a few days off. As far as I knew, all was going according to plan.

Then my phone rang. The head of Marine Public Affairs was on the other end of the line. "Ma'am," he said, employing the formal salutation I never quite got used to, "there's a story in the works."

A few months before, after Hagee was nominated, he had ordered his staff to investigate all of his medals to ensure he had the paperwork on hand to back them up. It was a routine precaution—a point of honor, and a matter of public relations smarts for a commander about to take a highly visible job.

The staff quickly turned up the paperwork to back up all the medals but three. No one seriously suspected bad faith on Hagee's part; one of the medals in question was the Vietnamese Cross of Gallantry, for example, and Hagee was widely known to have served heroically in Vietnam. This was a case of missing paperwork, pure and simple. The documentation was somewhere in the vast archives of the Marine Corps' records branch, and probably in Hagee's personal files as well, but the chances of its turning up before Hagee took over command of the Corps were slim.

Just to be safe, Hagee decided not to wear those decorations when he sat for his official photograph. But when the portrait was distributed to the press, an eagle-eyed reporter for *Stars and Stripes* compared it to an old photo of Hagee and noticed the discrepancy.

There was, of course, a clear explanation for Hagee's not wearing the medals. Still, the story had all the makings of a Washington scandal du jour: Hagee's opponents—he didn't have many, but everyone in power has some—could make it look as though a general about to take command of the Marine Corps, arguably the branch of the military most known for its devotion to honor, had been caught having worn medals he didn't earn. A similar allegation had, in fact, driven Admiral Jeremy "Mike" Boorda, the chief of naval operations, to suicide just a few years before.

The story was about to break by the time the Marine public affairs officer briefed me.

"Does the SecDef know?" I asked, using the Pentagon shorthand for Rumsfeld.

"No."

"Don't let him hear it from somebody else," I warned.

Not long after that call, Hagee and I were standing in Rumsfeld's office as Hagee explained the situation. When he finished, Rumsfeld turned to me.

"What do you think?"

"It could be a problem," I said, stating the obvious. Not an effective tactic with Rumsfeld.

"What do you *think we should do*?" he shot back.

We had plenty of options. We could, for example, have let the story sit with *Stars and Stripes* and hope it didn't go any further. Or Hagee could strike a defiant tone. Neither, I believed, would work.

"Sir," I replied, "I think General Hagee should brief a large group of the media and explain this himself before somebody else does."

The lighting is dim in the SecDef's office, but I think the blood drained from Hagee's face. This Marine, who served in Vietnam and Somalia, was awash in anxiety at the prospect of facing a room full of reporters. That reaction was understandable but, as it turned out, groundless. To his credit, Hagee held a briefing within hours, explained the decision to remove the medals, answered every question directly and honestly, and made no excuses for the mix-up. For their part, the Pentagon press corps was tough but generally respectful. The coverage was thorough but, for the most part, not sensational.

The *New York Times* coverage was a scant 239 words, and the lead sentence captured the story in a simple and nonhyped way: "The incoming commandant of the Marine Corps, Lt. Gen. Michael W. Hagee, said today that he had stopped wearing three military decorations because he and top aides could not find the documentation for the awards," Eric Schmitt wrote. Given how bad the story could have been, not bad.

A few others wrote more, but they gave play to Hagee's stand-up behavior.

Describing the process by which one documents commendations, Hagee said, as quoted in the third paragraph of Vern Loeb's *Washington Post* story, "I should have been more aggressive, and I should have had this done much sooner."

All the stories made sure readers knew that Secretary Rumsfeld had issued a statement giving Hagee his strongest backing.

A few days later, probably with a few more gray hairs, Hagee became commandant of the Marine Corps.

McCain's and Hagee's stories are less remarkable for what happened than for what never occurred: spin. All they did was go straight to the press and tell their stories. There was a time when it might have been different, when the last thing someone in their position would have done was volunteer to go before the press and lay out all the facts—unvarnished, untainted, unspun. Chances are a mouthpiece would have been dispatched to do the talking. If the "principal" had appeared personally, every word would have been poll-tested in advance, the timing of the news conference precision-calibrated to hit just the right moment in the news cycle, and questions planted with friendly reporters.

That's no longer true, or at any rate, it shouldn't be. Information travels too quickly. Sunshine permeates every corner of public and corporate life. A public figure who tries to hide from it is bound to be exposed—not just for what he or she has done, but for being unwilling to face it.

Because they faced the issues squarely, McCain and Hagee came out of the flare-ups with their integrity not only intact but enhanced. Reporters respected them for facing the music and telling the truth. Their approach could be summarized as a three-part strategy:

- Own up. McCain shouldn't have met with regulators in the first place, and he said so. Denying the obvious would have cost McCain the credibility he needed to fend off the charges that were genuinely unfair. Similarly, even if it clearly existed, Hagee should have had the documentation for the medals in hand before he ever put the medals on. By saying that openly, he avoided a round-robin of stories picking apart his denials.
- Stand up. McCain admitted what he *did* do, but he didn't engage in confessional politics. He rebutted unfair charges with a simple message that could be repeated ad nauseam: "I never asked any regulator to back off Keating." Hagee explained forcefully that while he took responsibility for not having the documentation, the medals *were* genuine.
- Speak up. McCain and Hagee spoke up early and often. No matter what's being alleged, *charges unanswered are charges assumed to be true.* Most important, they spoke up *personally.* Had they sent a staffer like me out to do the talking, they would have looked like they were hiding. By putting themselves on the line, McCain and Hagee let people know they were the kind of leaders who took responsibility for their actions and who weren't afraid of the truth.

Of course, the McCain and Hagee stories were simplified by the fact that, at bottom, they really hadn't done anything wrong.

Sometimes, though, you do just plain blow it. And on those occasions, it's more important than ever to do the talking yourself. Take it from someone who has gotten it wrong as many times as she's gotten it right. This tradition reaches so far back into my past, in fact, that the very first sound bite of my career was none other than these eloquent words, doubtless destined for eternal remembrance in *Bartlett's Familiar Quotations*:

"I screwed up."

It was my first political campaign. I was press secretary for Kansas congressional candidate Morris Kay in 1982, and I was on the front page of the *Topeka Capital Journal* acknowledging that I had misrepresented my candidate's views on Social Security. I must have missed the staff meeting on Social Security, because in some hastily written—and unapproved—press release, I left the senior citizens of northeastern Kansas with the distinct impression that "Mo" was going to ruin their retirements.

Morris Kay had bigger problems than me, like a very talented opponent, Jim Slattery, who went on to win. But he was very kind to me. For starters, he didn't fire me. Secondly, he laughed about it after I held an impromptu press conference before the Topeka press corps to admit my mistake.

"That wasn't too bad, was it?" he asked when I crawled back to the campaign headquarters down the street.

"I guess not," I mumbled. And then I went into the bathroom and threw up.

Now, you'd think apologizing on the front page and throwing up in the campaign office would have taught me a lesson. But ten years later, I was still at it. On the 1992 Bush-Quayle campaign, I seemed to find myself apologizing a lot. For referring to women as "chicks" (I thought you could do that if you were the youngest of five girls). For suggesting that then candidate Bill Clinton had so little national security experience he thought B-52s were a rock group. For referring to then President Bush as "studly" when he rode on a fire truck, as compared to Michael Dukakis in his infamous tank ride.

All of those comments paled in comparison to what I said about Pat Buchanan. We were heading into the Republican Convention after a tough primary season, thanks to Pat Buchanan's aggressive pounding on the president. Ross Perot was in the wings waiting to cause trouble, and even though the economy had started to improve, the public perception was just the opposite. All in all, it was a cranky time.

Conflict being the name of their game, the White House press corps and other political pundits were salivating at the thought of what Pat Buchanan's role might or might not be at the Republican Convention. Let him speak despite the fact he had said some pretty nasty things about the president? Keep him out and further alienate the right wing of the party, already distrustful of the president?

Those decisions were being made at a much higher pay grade than mine. What I did have to do, however, was endlessly repeat our mantra when asked if Buchanan would speak at the convention:

"Those speaking at the convention will be supporters of the president," we would utter—with a somewhat straight face—to the hundreds of reporters asking. This went on for weeks.

Labels on some prescriptions warn users against operating heavy machinery when under the influence of certain drugs. One mattress ad campaign highlights the importance of getting a good night's sleep. Neither drugs nor sleeplessness was my excuse the night that George Condon of Copley News Service called.

Just a couple of months before the Houston convention, George, a real pro, was doing his version of the "will he/won't he" story on Buchanan and the convention. Here's the part of the conversation on which George and I agree:

George: "So Torie, will Pat be speaking in Houston? Will he get a prime-time slot?"

Me, answering robotically as I sifted through other phone messages and notes on my desk: "Anyone speaking at the convention will be a supporter of the president."

George: "Come on. Really. Will he be there?"

Me: "All speakers at the convention will be supporters of the president." I knew the slight change in wording wouldn't get me anywhere with George, but I was sick of hearing myself say the same thing over and over again. But I did. George and I repeated ourselves about six times until we were both laughing. Here's where our version of the story differs:

George: "Come on, Torie. One last time. Will Pat Buchanan be a speaker in Houston?"

Me (laughing): "All right. Here's my real, off-the-record answer: he has to get down on his hands and knees and grovel on broken glass with his mouth open and his tongue hanging out—and then we'll talk."

George (laughing): "Great. Talk to you later."

George says I never said the off-the-record-part. I say I did. It doesn't matter. I never should have made the comment—even in jest.

About seven the next morning, I got a call from a friend, clearly concerned.

"You really have a death wish, don't you?" he asked me. And then he gave me the awful news that my quote about glass and knees and Pat's tongue was on the front page of the *San Diego Union-Tribune*.

My stomach churned, and I swore at myself for about a minute. And then I started writing the apologies—first to President Bush, for yet another mistake on my part that added to his heartburn, and then to Pat Buchanan, for having uttered one of the more tasteless comments that year.

"Please know that if anyone should be groveling it should be this press secretary" was part of my apology to Buchanan.

It's hard to believe, but reading my words on the front page of the paper wasn't even the worst part of the day. That came a little bit later when I asked a young fellow on the staff, Matt DeCamera, to hand-deliver the letter to Pat Buchanan. It was still early in the day. If I groveled enough, maybe we could minimize the impact of the follow-up stories that would start erupting as others in the press corps heard about Condon's piece.

"Bad news," Matt blurted out when he ran into my office less than an hour after heading out to deliver the letter. "Buchanan is at the Washington Hospital Center right now, and he's going to have open heart surgery today," he said, wasting no time getting to the point.

"Oh my God" is all I could think and say for a while. Now I felt really bad, and not for myself. "He could die on the operating table and the last thing he'll have heard is my nasty comments," I groaned. Adrenaline and panic took over. Now I cared less about what the president would think and more about Pat Buchanan's health and well-being. I shoved the letter and some cash for a cab into Matt's hands.

"Get yourself to the Washington Hospital Center and don't leave unless you've gotten this letter to him," I said as I pushed him toward the elevator. Ever resourceful, he did manage to make it into the pre-op ward at the Washington Hospital Center and tracked down Bay Buchanan, Pat's sister. Proving the Buchanan family had more class than I did, Bay Buchanan called me within an hour.

"Don't worry," she said to me as I mumbled rambling apologies over the phone. "I read your letter to Pat. He laughed and joked that he's said worse things."

Pat Buchanan survived surgery, thank God. I didn't get fired. Life went on. Now, I know what you're thinking. We had the Morris Kay campaign in 1982. The Buchanan disaster in 1992. Surely by 2002, I'd learned my lesson, right? Well, in a manner of speaking. Because the lesson I'd learned by then was to apologize quickly and honestly. But the mistakes? Those kept coming.

Like many people during the first few months after 9/11, I spent far more hours at the Pentagon than anywhere else. This is not a complaint, just reality. So often people would ask me how I put up with the pressure and the hours and with being away from my family. "Easy," I'd reply. "I think of the many men and women in uniform—doing the hard work. I get to go home at night. I get to sleep in my own bed and see my kids. They are asleep a lot when I see them, but I do get to see them, unlike the many deployed fathers and mothers away from home for months at a time." I had the easy job, I always thought. Heck, nobody was shooting at me.

December was upon us in no time. And though I could not figure out how to factor in time for my father's birthday or my husband's, both early in the month, I was bound and determined to make my daughter's. She was turning five on December 5, and birthdays at that age are a big deal.

The day started out badly. A B-52 flying in support of opposition forces north of Kandahar had dropped its ordnance near friendly forces some twelve hours earlier. Three U.S. Special Forces members were killed and another nineteen U.S. military were wounded. Five Afghans operating with our forces were killed as well, and scores more injured.

Rear Admiral John D. "Boomer" Stufflebeam, a deputy director of operations for the Joint Staff, and I briefed the media on the incident that day. We had few details, and the press was frustrated at our inability to state precisely what had happened. "You also need to appreciate that as a close air support mission, this is one of the potentially most hazardous types of missions that we use as a military tactic," Stufflebeam said. "Calling in air strikes nearly simultaneously on your own position, on enemy forces that you're engaged in close proximity to, is a hazardous business and takes very fine control and coordination and precision. And this is, I think, illustrative of what we have seen in training when sometimes things just don't work out perfectly."

Friendly fire accidents do occur—less than in the past, but they're still inevitable. And they're tragic. The veteran Pentagon correspondents understand that and tend not to overdramatize what is already a terrible event. The briefing skittered about that day. In addition to the friendly fire incident, we were dealing with a controversy over a request by a Navy reservist's family to have him buried in Arlington with his father. A female Air Force officer had also filed suit to protest Central Command's policy that women service members in Saudi Arabia wear the *abaya*—the pullover dress Muslim women wear to safeguard their modesty—when off base.

About halfway through the briefing we got the first hint of what was to come. But I missed the clue.

> *Q: Torie, this morning the pool reporters were ordered to*
> *stay in their quarters during the transfer of casualties to*
> *Rhino base. Can you explain why the only media in*
> *Afghanistan was kept away from that situation?*

My answer was a truthful one.

> *Clarke: I actually just don't have much information on it.*
> *I know I've gotten an e-mail or two from a couple of*
> *reporters. So we're looking into what the circumstances*
> *were. Clearly, there was a lot going on.*

The briefing went back to lots of questions—many of them hypothetical—about how the friendly fire incident happened.

The last question of the briefing was raised as a "housekeeping" issue.

> *Q: I know that you may not know what the exact*
> *circumstances were at Camp Rhino, where it's reported*
> *that, in fact, U.S. pool members were locked up and kept*
> *away from covering the treatment for—the medevac*
> *treatment for—these soldiers that were injured. But is it*
> *the Defense Department/Pentagon policy to prevent*
> *media coverage of any U.S. military killed or injured?*
> *Clarke: No.*

> *Q: And if such an event occurred, would the Pentagon try*
> *to rectify that situation?*

That question put me in a tough spot. A pretty good rule of thumb for dealing with the media is never to answer questions that start with "if." They're hypothetical. Had I accepted the presumption of the question, I would seem to be acknowledging that the event did occur. Maybe it did, but I didn't know yet. So I reverted to another rule of thumb: every question is an opportunity to present your message. I tried to answer by stating the Pentagon's policy:

> *Clarke: What we will try—what we try to do, and what we*
> *will continue to try to do, is provide access and facilitate*
> *media coverage of this very unconventional war. If*
> *something could impede or hinder operational security*
> *or could put lives at risk, then we will not let something*
> *go forward. But as a general course, as a general*
> *principle, what we're trying to do is facilitate coverage.*
> *And we would not—again, I—let's not talk about*
> *specifics here, because we don't know. But as a general*
> *principle, we want to facilitate coverage, and we will.*
> *Q: So you really have no information right now that any*
> *reporters were impeding anything or—*
> *Clarke: Right. I've just gotten a couple—I just got a couple*
> *of calls on it, and we haven't had a chance to run it*
> *down. But I will.*

I didn't. And that was the first big mistake of the day.

After the briefing, numerous other issues rose up, as they

19

always did. I was busy. With the birthday party coming up, a pressing question on my mind was whether I had confirmed Nancy Edson, the puppet lady. I did not get pinged again on the reporters' being denied access at Rhino. It never crossed my mind again. Driving home, I did think about those who had been killed and injured in the friendly fire incident. I thought about their families as I drove home to mine in suburban Maryland.

The party was in full swing by six p.m. Fifteen five-year-olds packed full of sugar were enjoying Nancy's innovative rendition of "The Frog Prince in Japan," a fairy tale. Just as I was giving myself a mental pat on the back for my multitasking abilities, all hell broke loose. My pager, cell phone, home phone, and secure phone upstairs went off simultaneously.

The page was from Army Colonel George Rhynedance, my senior military assistant. Like all of Rhynedance's messages, this one was to the point: "Have problem. Call."

The caller ID number on my cell was one I recognized immediately as a major bureau chief with whom I spoke frequently.

The secure call was from Cables, the Pentagon communications system. Rhynedance had them call me just in case I didn't have my pager on. "We're not positive yet," Rhynedance said when I called in, "but we think we may, indeed, have barred the media from covering the victims' return at Rhino."

No way, I thought. Nobody would do that. Policy and practice dictate that when horrible friendly fire incidents happen in combat, the news media should be allowed to cover them, with consideration given to the next of kin.

"Get as much as you can by way of ground truth from Rhino and call me back," I yelled over the din of the birthday party.

Next, I dialed the bureau chief, a serious sort who never called with idle complaints.

"Do you know that some of your guys locked the reporters in a box at Rhino so they couldn't cover the friendly fire victims?" the bureau chief asked.

"I find that really hard to believe," I said. "But I'll check it out and get back to you." I hoped it wasn't true, but I was beginning to think the worst.

The phones rang nonstop for the next forty-five minutes, and the complaint was the same from all: "Your guys put the media in a box." It had taken a few hours for the reporters at Rhino to reach their editors back in the States, but the trickle of questions at the earlier briefing was now a torrent of accusations.

The first problem was lingo: the Marines at Camp Rhino wouldn't call it a box. They would call it a room, admittedly a small room; some called it a warehouse. And, although I never saw it, several there told me it was a room with no windows. Whatever it was, a well-meaning officer did what 99 percent of us would do in the same situation. When he saw the victims coming back into Rhino, he immediately thought of their families. He didn't want anybody back home seeing their loved ones on TV or in a photograph before the military had notified them. So he kept the media away—good intentions, but flatly contrary to policy.

But the big failures were mine—on several levels. First of all, I did not anticipate what might happen when a friendly fire incident did occur. They are an unfortunate part of life in the military. We worked hard every day to improve Pentagon policy on so many aspects of this new and unconventional war. I should have thought through what we would do when friendly fire happened. I didn't.

Second, I didn't pick up on the early clues. The news media—especially the longtime Pentagon correspondents—get better information than just about anybody. And they often get it sooner. I should have paid more attention to the questions and e-mails I got that morning and during the briefing.

Finally, if you say you're going to follow up on something, follow up. I left the briefing, tackled other issues, and then headed home, despite having committed before the Pentagon press corps to get to the bottom of the issue.

I deserved every bit of grief I got throughout the rest of the day, the night—and the next morning. You know the day will be bad when your first call from outside the building is Howard Kurtz of the *Washington Post*. Howie writes about the media and frequently points out—accurately—the challenges of managing the often antagonistic relationship between the news media and the government. Calling back a fellow who writes about the media is not—in my book—as important as working with the media who cover you, but Howie has great radar. And he has a keen sense for a real controversy. He's also a nice guy. I called him back.

"People are furious," he said, stating the obvious.

"No kidding," I said. "And they have every right to be. What happened goes against policy and all our training. It shouldn't have happened, and we'll fix it." I wasn't sure right then how we would fix it, but this time I was determined to follow up on my commitment. By late that morning we had followed up. We e-mailed and faxed to all bureau chiefs a letter from me.

We owe you an apology. The last several days have revealed severe shortcomings in our preparedness to support news organizations in their efforts to cover U.S. military operations in Afghanistan.

We have a significant responsibility to provide your correspondents the opportunity to cover the war. It is a responsibility that we take seriously. Our policy remains the same as it always has been: Keeping in mind our desire to protect operational security and the safety of men and women in uniform, we intend to provide maximum media coverage with minimal delay and hassle. That has not always been the case over the last few days, particularly with regard to the coverage of dead and wounded returning to the Forward Operating Base known as Rhino.

The letter went on to describe the actions we took to address the problems. They included assigning more senior staff to handle media logistics in the theater, and reissuing guidance that clearly expressed our intent, "maximum coverage, minimum hassle."

It ended with a statement of a very sincere belief and a commitment that became even more critical in the months ahead:

The road ahead will not be easy. While we cannot do everything you might want in covering this most unconventional of wars, we can guarantee one thing: we will keep the lines of communication with you open at all times to address these and other issues.

Many in the news media gave us points for admitting past mistakes but made clear their skepticism that we'd improve going forward.

"We appreciate the Pentagon is willing to recognize that this

the precise word typically employed—the day before, a well-meaning Defense Protective Service (DPS) officer had arrested Fox cameraman Greg Gursky and held him briefly for taking footage of what looked like a suspicious traffic stop on Route 110 next to the Pentagon. It was against DPS rules—prominently posted all over the Pentagon—to take unauthorized photos or video while physically on the "reservation," as the grounds are called.

Briefing with me that day was Air Force Brigadier General John W. Rosa Jr., deputy director for current operations on the Joint Staff. Rosa and I often argued good-naturedly about who got to brief what. The more news you could deliver, the less of a punching bag you were during the briefing. On this day, given my concerns with the "too good to be true" aspects of this story, I was more than happy to let Rosa do the honors on the G. Gordon front. No profile in courage, I know.

After my brief remarks on the Fort Drum accident and some comments on the military commissions, Rosa launched into the discovery.

> Rosa: While our forces were searching one cave in the Anaconda area on Monday, they discovered a hand-held GPS, Global Positioning System unit. The GPS had the name "G. Gordon" on it. We currently believe this GPS belonged to Army Master Sergeant Gary Gordon, an Army Special Ops Force soldier killed in Somalia in 1993. Sergeant Gordon was honored with the Medal of Honor for his actions in Somalia. And the Army's notified his family that this item has been found.

The announcement had the expected result. From the podium in the briefing room, I watched reporters' eyebrows arch upward in unison and saw their pencils start flying.

> Q: *For General Rosa, what significance do you place on the fact that this GPS equipment that was found that came from Somalia, what does that say about previous suspicions that al Qaeda was linked to the forces of Mohamed Aidid back in 1993 in Somalia?*

Usually it's nice when the reporters tee up *exactly* what you want to talk about, especially in briefings carried live. This time, we would come to regret it.

> Rosa: *That's a good question, one we've been doing some thought about. There are a couple of conclusions you may draw. First of all, we've said all along that we suspect that al Qaeda, being a worldwide network, and the fact that this piece we currently think originated from Somalia, would obviously tie—could obviously tie al Qaeda to Somalia.*

Rosa tried to qualify the information with that word "could." If I had been doing my job well that day I would have jumped in and underscored the qualification even more. I didn't. The news was all over TV within minutes. It didn't last long.

About an hour later, we heard from the *Army Times*. While many media were busily booking military experts and talking heads to speculate about the importance of the story, this fellow went to a more sophisticated source: the manufacturer. He learned that the GPS device in question wasn't manufactured until 1997, well after the Black Hawk incident in Somalia. "G. Gordon," it turned out, was the nickname of a soldier deployed in Afghanistan who had given the device to another who fought against al Qaeda in Operation Anaconda, one of the largest military offensives in Afghanistan.

Ouch.

I groaned, kicked myself for not heeding my instincts, and got to work. Just talking with the *Army Times* wouldn't be enough. This news too was bound to get out. And more than a few journalists joined us in rushing to get the story out. They looked bad as well, and some of them might take it out on us. We had to fix this one ourselves.

I told the staff to draft a statement admitting the mistake. "Make it short, and don't make excuses," I said. "Just say we screwed up and get the correct information out. And make sure Gary Gordon's family knows." Then I hightailed it to Rumsfeld's office to fill him in. The last thing we needed was for Rumsfeld to hear it from someone else before he knew the whole story.

Rumsfeld rolled his eyes. "Clean it up," he ordered. That's one of Rumsfeld's cardinal rules: when you screw up, fix it and fix it fast. During Rumsfeld's own briefings, he encouraged us to interrupt him—right there in front of reporters and, often, a live TV audience—if he made a mistake.

The moment the statement was ready, we released it, posted it on the DOD Web site, and sent it to thousands nationwide by blast e-mail and fax. When a transcript of the morning's briefing was posted on the Pentagon's Web site, we inserted the statement in brackets. "DOD Clarifies Origin of GPS System," the release headline read. "Initial indications that the GPS unit potentially belonged to a U.S. servicemember killed in Somalia several years ago have now been determined to be inaccurate," we stated briefly. We explained how the GPS device in question found its way to Afghanistan, quite innocently, it turned out. It wasn't the kind of media story I like to see, but it was over quickly, and some reporters went out of their way to compliment our candor in admitting our screwup.

At first glance, our strategy may sound counterintuitive. React to questions about the mistakes, sure. Explain the facts, absolutely. But why would the Pentagon go out of its way to *announce* bad news? The reason is simple: in the Information Age, the bad news is going to get out. The only questions are who will tell it first and will they tell it accurately.

The same rule applies in the business world, politics, or anywhere else. Wait for somebody else to tell the story, and you're probably not going to like how they tell it. Try to stonewall or blur the truth? Your competitors and the media that cover you will eat you for lunch. If reporters believe they've caught you doing something you were hoping to hide, the coverage is magnified by a factor of ten. If you leave off the details—or, worse, mislead the audience—you'll turn a one-day story into several days of follow-ups, every one of which will both repeat the bad news one more time and, to ice the cake, accuse you of having lied about it too. What seemed at first like an honest attempt to come clean will end up looking like a deceptive manipulation scheme.

And don't expect too much glory for coming clean about

bad news. A bad story is still a bad story. One of the most common mistakes people communicating with the public make is treating the media like underlings whose job is to do what you tell them. The fact that you come clean doesn't mean they aren't going to cover what went wrong in the first place. They're supposed to. Remember, they don't call it "taking your lumps" for nothing. But it's a heck of a lot better to take them on your own terms.

And telling the truth yourself does have its benefits. Most reporters thought more highly of McCain after the Keating Five scandal than they did before. That's where the national media first caught on to the fact that he's a straight talker. Admitting mistakes—or delivering your own bad news—can be a fine example of turning the customer. Ask Michael Phelps.

The six-time Olympic gold swimming medalist is either a communications genius or someone who got good advice when he was charged with drunk driving in the fall of 2004. Within a few days of his arrest, Phelps was calling media outlets all over the place with a simple, straightforward, no-excuses statement: "I'm sorry."

"Last week I made a mistake," Phelps said in a prepared statement. "Getting into a vehicle after anything to drink is wrong, dangerous, and unacceptable." Appearing at a Baltimore health and fitness exposition just a few days after the incident, Phelps took multiple questions from reporters before signing autographs. "I wanted to look people in the eye and tell them that I made a mistake. I want to reach out and affect as many people as I can." He appeared on the *Today* show the following Monday and repeated the core message: "The mistake that I made is a big mistake. This is something that—every single morning I wake up and I look at myself in the mirror and I have to live with the mistake that I made."

Reputation and endorsements at stake, Phelps chose the best course of action and executed it flawlessly. And it paid off. His fans—always loyal—seemed even more impressed with him after. Before the incident, I didn't know a lot about Phelps. Afterwards, I saw him as an honest kid who took responsibility for his mistakes. As Daniel de Vise reported in the *Washington Post* following Phelps's Baltimore appearance, "In this crowd, there was nothing but sympathy."

In a similar vein, here's a counterintuitive notion for you: the best thing Martha Stewart ever did for her reputation was go to jail. Don't get me wrong: all things considered, it would have been best had she not gotten into trouble to start with. But once she was convicted, volunteering to go to jail even though her case was on appeal was a masterstroke. It showed her as human and vulnerable—the exact opposite of the superior ice queen the media savaged her as being. And even though she continued pursuing her appeals, she was still taking responsibility— quite refreshing in the storm of finger-pointing that followed other corporate scandals.

When Leona Helmsley got out of prison, her hotel chain came up with one of the best marketing lines ever. "Say what you will," the glossy ads in high end magazines said, "she runs a helluva hotel." Rather than dodge the obvious, Leona embraced her problems and made them—sort of—a positive.

Say what you will about Martha Stewart, and I know next to nothing about what she did that put her in the slammer for six months, but she knows how to tell her own story, even under the toughest of circumstances. As soon as charges flew that she may have broken the law, Martha and her team launched a Web site called marthatalks.com. Simple and straightforward, it was Martha's side of the story in her own—and sometimes her lawyers'—words. The site included "Notes to Martha," expressions of support sent in by friends and fans, "Other Voices," excerpts of editorials and reporting favorable to her case, and even "Trial Update," a section devoted to briefs and substantive updates on the trial's progress.

By the time Stewart entered the West Virginia prison nicknamed Camp Cupcake, Martha Stewart Omnimedia and the famous TV show producer Mark Burnett were workng on a couple of TV shows for her when she got out, and the company's stock price was up. Greg Schneider of the *Washington Post* called it an example of "raw, stubborn survival" in a 2004 year-end piece headlined "Martha, like Deficits and SUVs, Showed Staying Power."

I called it exceptional communications skill. Tell your own story and don't hide from the obvious. At their best, statements from CEOs are usually murky. But Stewart's statements on marthatalks.com were straight to the point. Even her preholiday letter posted at the end of 2004 made no attempt to disguise her whereabouts: "When one is incarcerated with 1,200 other inmates, it is hard to be selfish at Christmas. . . . So many of the women here at Alderson will never have the joy and wellbeing that you and I experience. Many of them have been here for years—devoid of care, devoid of love, devoid of family."

Stewart neither sought nor seemed to want sympathy. Her Christmas letter focused on her fellow inmates and her newfound views on sentencing and prison reform, not her personal predicament. Was Stewart's prison-era PR program self-serving?

Absolutely. But it was also in the best interests of the company and its shareholders. Stewart's team deserves credit for developing a comprehensive and aggressive program to help her recover from a serious setback. She deserves more credit for having the guts to execute it. And while she may not have sought sympathy, that's exactly what her honesty got her.

"I am confident that you will come through this with dignity and that in the spring you will be back to business as usual," wrote one fan. That letter expressed a common theme, that Martha got more than she deserved from the prosecutors. "We feel it is a travesty of justice that such a fine lady as yourself should have to serve time when hardened criminals are let go on technicalities every day. If it were up to us, you would never serve one day."

I doubt Stewart's company manufactured the fans' notes. They didn't have to. Stewart has her critics, to be sure, but many admire what she did with her company. And many of them weren't going to abandon her when things looked bad.

The pharmaceutical giant Merck seemingly employed a similarly straightforward approach in 2004 when they had to pull their high-selling arthritis drug Vioxx after studies showed that its users faced an increased risk of heart attack and stroke. Hum "It's a Beautiful Day" and you'll remember their omnipresent ads even now. Pulling the drug wasn't the hardest part: the hardest part was figuring out how to tell so many audiences—customers, physicians, and policy makers among them—while maintaining the credibility of the company as well as confidence in its other drugs.

Merck could have taken the easy path, and a decade or more ago, they might have: just let the media cover the story. The

Vioxx study was everywhere, so it wasn't as though Merck had to be the ones to deliver the news, and no one could have blamed them had they not wanted to. This was devastating news about one of their most important products. According to Merck, some 2 million people worldwide used Vioxx at the time of the announcement; about 84 million had used it since it came on the marketplace in 1999. Literally millions of people were impacted by the news. No spin, no bluster, no fancy words could get around that. Merck execs took what looked like—at first blush—the better approach, an up-front and forward-leaning one.

In announcing their decision to pull Vioxx, Merck head Ray V. Gilmartin said, "We're taking the action because we believe it best serves the interests of the patients."

Call me cynical, but the decision also best served the company's interests. Already hit with a lawsuit by a Missouri woman who claimed her daughter was misled about the potential risks of Vioxx and died as a result, the company was clearly worried about additional lawsuits and the enormous toll—on their finances and reputation—of drawn-out litigation. No matter what the reasons, Merck handled the decision and the accompanying communications challenges well. The first day, they had senior executives on several major cable shows to answer the many questions. Good for them, I thought.

I'd lay a bet, by the way, that some of their lawyers were apoplectic over this strategy. With litigation pending, most lawyers counsel silence. They're fine people, and they're doing their jobs, which is to keep their clients out of trouble in the courtroom. But many a lawyer has protected his client in the courtroom at the expense of his reputation in the court of public opinion, and the punishments handed down in the latter are often far more damaging. In this case, I'd guess, Merck correctly calculated that the most serious risk the company faced was a loss of public confidence in its product.

According to the *Washington Post*'s David Brown, Vioxx accounted for slightly more than 10 percent of Merck's annual sales in 2003. A market research firm, IMS, estimated that Merck spent $500 million in 2003 promoting the drug to doctors through advertising, free samples, and visits to physicians' offices. Faced with perhaps its biggest challenge ever, the company spared little expense when it came to the damage control campaign.

Full-page ads in major national newspapers said it loud and clear:

> Merck & Co., Inc., announced today a voluntary withdrawal of VIOXX. This decision is based on new data from a three-year clinical study. In this study, there was an increased risk for cardiovascular (CV) events, such as heart attack and stroke, in patients taking VIOXX 25 mg compared to those taking placebo (sugar pill).

Merck said what they were doing and why, in a straightforward fashion and with no excuses. The full-page ads, as with most of the company's communications about pulling the drugs, also pointed patients and doctors to Web sites for more information—Web sites that, for the most part, were relatively straightforward.

The fact that Merck seemed to admit what was wrong gave them the initial credibility to refute charges that were inaccurate. Here too, they didn't count solely on the news media to carry the day for them. They used multiple communications vehicles, including Web sites and advertising, to address the more egregious charges. They reminded consumers and the medical community that they had "extensively studied" Vioxx before seeking regulatory approval and had taken steps to gather additional information about the medicine. Underscoring what clearly would be important in the legal challenges, the company stressed again that it had voluntarily withdrawn the drug from the market.

Merck's communications strategy wasn't a one-hit wonder. It was a comprehensive and sustained program to address the crisis. The strategy preserved the company's credibility in the early weeks of the crisis and may have even bolstered it, at least for a while. In a November 19, 2004, *New York Times* article, reporter Alex Berenson wrote that Merck CEO Gilmartin had received better than expected treatment when testifying before the Senate Finance Committee, partly because of how the company had handled the crisis once it broke.

"Merck as a company and Mr. Gilmartin personally can draw upon a reservoir of credibility that has not been available to many of the other companies that have come under fire," Berenson wrote. "His differences from other executives even extended to the way they testify. Where others came to Congress flanked by legions of lawyers and public relations experts, Mr. Gilmartin sat alone in front of the Committee." The headline over the article was one no spin doctor could ever buy: "For Merck Chief, Credibility at the Capitol." Credibility, I might add, that he may not have had before the tough story broke.

All good, right? Not exactly. As months went by and scrutiny continued, the fault line in the Merck PR plan became apparent. Despite the company's well-delivered public assurances about Vioxx's safety, reports surfaced that Merck had continued to market the heck out of Vioxx, even though internal research and outside studies suggested good reasons to be concerned about the drug's risks.

People who follow pharmaceutical companies far more closely than I do can and will find fault, I am sure, with many of the company's actions and motivations. From an outsider's perspective, it sure looks like there must have been more information than they shared with the public.

And the strategy took its toll. Barely six months after pulling Vioxx, Merck faced thousands of lawsuits, its stock price was some 60 percent off its peak, and CEO Gilmartin was forced into early retirement with a badly damaged reputation.

"For Mr. Gilmartin, yesterday's announcement ends years of failure," stated the May 6, 2005, *New York Times* story announcing Gilmartin's departure. "Mr. Gilmartin is widely liked personally, but his tenure at Merck has been little short of disastrous." The reporter who wrote the story? The same Alex Berenson who saw Gilmartin's credibility grow before Congress the previous fall.

The legal system will determine whether or not Merck's actions were wrong. As you face challenges and problems in your organization, know one thing for sure: no reservoir of credibility, no matter how deep, will sustain you if you lie or deliberately misinform. It's wrong for the obvious reasons, and it's stupid, too. Especially in this era, information will get out. Enterprising reporters will find it, often aided by disgruntled employees or those sincerely concerned about their organization's activities. Read the book *24 Days* by *Wall Street Journal* reporters Rebecca Smith and John R. Emshwiller about Enron's collapse to get a clear picture of how insiders will expose what they think needs to be exposed. Time after time, Enron employees offered the reporters important tips, documents, and background that helped guide their reporting, reporting that contributed significantly to Enron's downfall.

And thanks to the Internet, these days people don't even need reporters to get their information out publicly. With a few minutes and some keystrokes, they can let the whole world know what you might not want revealed.

If you ever hear yourself saying, "Don't worry, no one will ever find out," about something unpleasant in your organization, just slap yourself. Negative information will get out, one way or another. And no communications plan, no matter how well developed and flawlessly executed it might be, will save you if you're lying. The truth will come out.

For a great example of a CEO who admits his mistakes—not to mention for some good reading—peruse the annual Chairman's Letter from Warren Buffett to Berkshire Hathaway shareholders. Read just a few examples, and several things become apparent. One, Buffett embraces simplicity. He writes in clear, straightforward, and grammatically correct sentences. He makes important and insightful references to societal and economic factors that influence his decisions. He tells some good jokes—the kind you can tell your parents. And he admits mistakes.

As far back as the seventies, Buffett's letter is sprinkled with admissions of weakness, poor judgments, and miscalculations. "While our operating earnings per share were up 37% from the year before, our beginning capital was up 24%, making the gain in earnings per share considerably less impressive than it might appear at first glance." Buffett actually goes out of his way to highlight the caution in his 1977 letter. "We had mistakenly predicted better results in each of the last two years," he writes, describing their textile operations. Despite a downturn in all textiles nationwide, Buffett makes sure his shareholders know that "some of the problems have been of our own making."

The 1986 Chairman's Letter starts with a brief description of the company's net gain of 26.1% or $492.5 million, mostly crediting managers of the major operating businesses. And then Buffett wastes no time getting to the problems. "So much for the good news," he writes in just the fifth paragraph. "The bad news is that my performance did not match that of our managers. While they were doing a superb job in running our businesses, I was unable to skillfully deploy much of the capital they generated."

After describing one acquisition, that of a small company named Fechheimer, Buffett went on at length about his failings. "Meanwhile, we had no new ideas in the marketable equities field," according to Buffett. "So our main capital allocation moves in 1986 were to pay off debt and stockpile funds. Neither is a fate worse than death, but they do not inspire us to do handsprings either. If Charlie [his number two at Berkshire] and I were to draw blanks for a few years in our capital-allocation endeavors, Berkshire's rate of growth would slow significantly." So Buffett admits his big mistake for the year and wisely manages expectations going forward.

Adopting one of John McCain's favorite sayings, "May the words I utter today be sweet, for tomorrow I may have to eat them," Buffett acknowledges late in the letter that the company has bought a corporate jet. With a frank recitation of the plane's costs and an admission that it was *not* absolutely necessary, Buffett also recalls his past opposition to such purchases. "Your Chairman, unfortunately, has in the past made a number of rather intemperate remarks about corporate jets. Accordingly, prior to our purchase, I was forced into my Galileo mode. I promptly experienced the necessary 'counter-revelation' and travel is now considerably easier—and considerably costlier—than in the past. Whether Berkshire will get its money's worth from the plane is an open question, but I will work at achieving some business triumph that I can (no matter how dubiously) attribute to it."

I'll make you a bet that most shareholders didn't begrudge Buffett that plane—if only because they trust and appreciate him.

These statements also show that when Buffett admits mistakes, he takes on the responsibility himself rather than passing it along. The 2003 shareholder letter included—as usual—an understated and quick rundown on Berkshire's amazing progress. In the thirty-nine years of Buffett's management, Berkshire Hathaway's per share book value grew from $19 to over $50,000. Describing the common institutional pressures facing other organizations, Buffett points out that Berkshire, fortunately, was saddled with none of them. "At Berkshire, neither history nor the demands of owners impede intelligent decision-making. When Charlie and I make mistakes, they are—in tennis parlance—unforced errors."

Contrast that candor with the convoluted statements and brashness of Enron executives. Seasoned financial reporters covering Enron complained about the company's overly complicated and misleading statements, earnings reports, and explanations. Reporters struggled to get to the bottom of the company's complex and, as it quickly became apparent, improper financial transactions.

Even the savviest analysts were perplexed by some of the company's explanations, which caused them to have serious doubts about its future. Smith and Emshwiller recount an October 23, 2001, conference call designed to allay investors' concern over the SEC investigation and mounting negative stories. CEO Ken Lay and other Enron execs repeatedly dodged tough questions about the company's management of what looked like serious potential liabilities.

> But even longtime Enron fans were starting to have doubts. David Fleischer came on the line. The Goldman analyst offered not so much a question as a plea. "With all due respect," Fleischer said, a note of urgency in his voice, "you know what you are hearing from some of these people and many others that you haven't heard from on this call is that the company's credibility is being severely questioned and there really is a need for much more disclosure. . . .There is an appearance that you are hiding something."

Ken Lay's shareholder letters—especially compared to Warren Buffett's—were an exercise in exuberance and pomposity and certainly wouldn't address concerns like Fleischer's. Phrases like " astonishing success" and "enormous competitive advantages" and "unparalleled" filled the pages. In Lay's world, there were no downsides, no problems or challenges ahead. In short, no reality.

* * *

One of the best reasons to 'fess up early and completely is to move past a bad story. When you aren't forthright about your mistakes, stories dog you much longer than they need to. It's a lesson the Bush White House learned the hard way in the summer of 2003.

Think back to the now infamous "Mission Accomplished" banner that hung behind the president on the deck of the USS *Abraham Lincoln* when he announced that "major combat operations" were over. I had been pushing for senior officials to greet troops as they returned from combat. The first I heard of what became the *Lincoln* fiasco was when the White House called to ask my opinion about the president's flying to the West Coast to greet sailors returning home from duty.

"I think that'd be great," I replied. Then I rushed out the door to accompany Rumsfeld on an overseas trip. The next time I heard about it was when the whole world did. We were in Rumsfeld's hotel suite for a meeting when CNN International began showing images of the president jetting onto the deck of the *Lincoln,* emerging in a flight suit, and announcing that "major combat operations" in Iraq were over. In his defense, the president did go on to state that some of the toughest fighting might lie ahead, that there was much more hard work to be done, and that Iraq remained a dangerous place. I cringed, not least because I hadn't followed up with the White House on the event. No news is often good news, and since I hadn't heard anything from the White House about the president's trip, I had assumed everything was going swimmingly with the Navy on the plans for the event.

While the president's precise words were correct, the triumphal mood of the event—punctuated by the "Mission Accomplished" banner—left the impression that the administration was declaring victory in Iraq. For months, every subsequent story on Iraq reported the number of soldiers who had died there since the president had declared the end of major combat operations. Democrats accused the president of using the military as a political backdrop.

All in all, not a good story, but the White House, loath to admit it had fouled up, made matters worse. Their first explanation was that the sailors on the *Lincoln* had made the banner themselves without the White House's knowledge. Then the media figured out—surprise, surprise—that there were no printing facilities on board where a banner that size could have been made. At one point months later, the explanation was that the "mission" the banner said had been "accomplished" was just the *Lincoln*'s particular tour from which it was returning. Some said that the *Lincoln*'s crew had asked the White House to have the banner made. In the end, the White House grudgingly admitted that maybe that banner might not have been such a good idea. By that time, their credibility had sustained a hit, and their reputation for stubbornness had been ratcheted up a notch. Had they skipped straight to the apology, the effect might very well have been the opposite, and they would certainly have spared themselves a few days of heartburn in the interim.

When critics accuse the administration of refusing to admit obvious mistakes, Rumsfeld, as a senior member of the team, often gets painted with the same brush. Actually, he's better at admitting mistakes—and has a faster instinct for doing so—than anyone else I know. And early in his second run as secretary of defense, two events quickly triggered that instinct.

In the spring of 2001, China downed an American reconnaissance plane and took its twenty-four crewmembers prisoner on Hainan Island. A diplomatic standoff ensued as the Chinese and the United States argued—quietly—over the return of the crew and plane. Confusion broke out on April 30 when the Pentagon put out a statement that called for suspension of U.S.–China military contacts, even as the Bush administration worked hard to maintain the relationship and downplay the seriousness of the incident. The DOD statement was pulled a few hours after its release, and Rumsfeld accepted responsibility for the mistake even when most fingers pointed at an aide.

Appearing a few days later on CBS's *Face the Nation,* he said, "There's no question that I made a mistake. A mistake was made. To the extent there's any fault . . . to be assigned, it's certainly as much mine as anybody else's, and I'm in charge."

About the same time, Rumsfeld had picked a one-star flag officer as his senior military assistant. The selection raised eyebrows because most of the recent senior military assistants for secretaries had been two-stars or three-stars, a grade inflation, if you will, since Rumsfeld's previous stint as SecDef in the seventies. He wanted to "cool things down," so he chose Rear Admiral J. J. Quinn. Quinn gave the job his best 24/7, but it was hard for a one-star to command the influence he needed to manage the front office's interaction with three-stars, four-stars, and senior civilians. Rumsfeld and Quinn talked it over and decided, together, that the best thing to do was to get a three-star. When *Washington Post* reporter Tom Ricks asked about the decision and the rumors swirling around it, Rumsfeld stepped up to the plate. "It turned out I made a mistake, just to be blunt about it, thinking that a one-star could, simply, because he was in the secretary's office, get the place to move at the same pace that a three-star could or a two-star," Rumsfeld said in the May 17, 2001, interview. "And I guess it was just an honest mistake on my part."

By admitting the mistake early, Rumsfeld helped the whole building move past the problem more quickly. Quinn, as the secretary called him, "is absolutely first-rate" and wound up in charge of a carrier strike group—a far better job, some might say, than the one he had.

A willingness to admit something stinks is a powerful tool. In fact, doing exactly that made one of the toughest tasks in Washington—closing excess military bases—a lot easier. That process is run by the Base Realignment and Closure Commission, created in 1988 to deal with the reality and the ever-present politics of U.S. military facilities that are obsolete or redundant—in short, not needed.

Not needed, that is, unless you're a citizen or the mayor or the local congressman from that area. Over the years, many people in these communities have become very attached to their bases for financial, emotional, and political reasons. Closing them, despite reams of quantifiable evidence that they no longer serve a useful purpose to the military, became next to impossible because of the political pressure put on the military, Congress, and administrations.

The problem has bedeviled administrations going back to JFK and Defense Secretary Robert McNamara, accused of closing bases for—what else—political reasons, to punish congressional opponents. Aggrieved congressmen passed several pieces of legislation making it impossible for the president to eliminate facilities without their approval. Finally, in the mid-1980s, Senator Barry Goldwater (R-Ariz.) and Defense Secretary Caspar Weinberger marshaled forces to reduce excess military infrastructure. They created the first BRAC commission, from which the rest have taken their direction. Four "rounds" of base-closing efforts thus far have closed dozens of large bases and hundreds of small ones and saved—by some estimates—more than $25 billion.

BRAC, supposedly, would make the necessary yet distasteful task nonpolitical by appointing commission members beholden to no one except the American taxpayer. The commission members review and analyze a list of bases submitted by the Pentagon for possible closure or realignment and make their recommendations. The president and Congress must accept the whole package or send it back to the commission, which prevents political cherry-picking.

The theory is great, but the practical execution is far tougher. Despite every best intention to make decisions in a politics- and pressure-free zone, human nature takes over. Politicians, residents, retired military, and casts of thousands at PR firms spend millions of dollars on campaigns to influence decision makers back in Washington.

There have been four BRAC commission rounds thus far. And each time, those in charge at the Pentagon have tried to make the best of it by making the process seem palatable to the communities involved. Not Rumsfeld. "It is not something that anyone with any sense wants to go and do," Rumsfeld said in a Pentagon press briefing in early August 2001. "I mean, if you get up in the morning and ask yourself how you want to spend your time, that is not how you want to spend your time, running around up on Capitol Hill talking about closing bases in people's congressional districts and in their states."

Or, as his special assistant, Larry Di Rita, put it more succinctly in a meeting later that day, "You can put a lot of lipstick on that pig, but it's still a pig." Larry always has a way of getting to the point—quickly.

The effect of this new—reality-based—approach to BRAC was impressive. First, just the honesty of it made the whole process less distasteful. Instead of everybody's trying to cast matters in a light they thought palatable to the other side, everyone just called it what it was—a very difficult process. In and of itself, that made the effort more constructive. Secondly, it was a huge time-saver. Instead of hundreds of staffers spending thousands of man-hours on the impossible task of trying to craft initiatives and messages that would somehow make BRAC more appealing, we spent that time on the substance of BRAC and other pressing business.

Sometimes, how you talk about something makes a difference. Other times—as with BRAC—it matters little what you say or even how you say it.

That's certainly the case with Abu Ghraib, the scandal involving abuse of Iraqi prisoners by U.S. military personnel. I hesitate to talk about it, because the story broke months after I left the Pentagon. I don't know all the details. I know that I can't possibly know everything, despite the heavy media coverage.

But I know enough to put the issue firmly in the category of a pig. At the end of the day, no matter what factors you consider—and there were many that contributed to what happened at Abu Ghraib—some human beings did horrible things to other human beings. No matter what crimes and atrocities those prisoners may have committed, they did not deserve the abuse, torture, and harassment they received. You can't get around that.

Should there have been better supervision of the MPs who participated in the abuse? *Absolutely.* Could civilian and military leadership have sounded alarm bells sooner at the first sign of possible abuse? Perhaps, but for the record, it *was* Central Command that first made the investigation public, not the news media.

On January 16, 2004, as part of his daily briefing, then Brigadier General Mark Kimmitt, deputy director for coalition operations in Baghdad, announced an investigation into reports of detainee abuse.

CentCom issued a statement that day that said all they could at the time:

DETAINEE TREATMENT INVESTIGATION

BAGHDAD, Iraq—An investigation has been initiated into reported incidents of detainee abuse at a Coalition Forces detention facility. The release of specific information concerning the incidents could hinder the investigation, which is in its early stages. The investigation will be conducted in a thorough and professional manner. The Coalition is committed to treating all persons under its control with dignity, respect and humanity. Lt. Gen. Ricardo S. Sanchez, the Commanding General, has reiterated this requirement to all members of CJTF-7.

Should Rumsfeld and others have demanded more answers earlier in the process? Ideally, yes, but practically, they couldn't. Had they become more involved, even asking private questions, they might have biased possible prosecutions. The lawyers at CentCom and in the Pentagon were adamant that no one, especially people like Rumsfeld high up in the chain of command, say or do anything that could be perceived as "command influence," given the ongoing investigations and likely prosecutions.

I understand their intent, but I still think the policy is mistaken. In my mind, there's clearly something wrong with a policy that doesn't allow a secretary of defense to reach down into the system and fix something that's gone horribly wrong, but that was the policy, and Rumsfeld and other higher-ups were bound by it.

Many said that once the news media started covering the story, the Pentagon should "come clean," release "all" the photos and any other allegations of prisoner abuse that had not already come to light. Under most circumstances, that would have been good advice. But the only thing worse than what happened at Abu Ghraib would have been the perpetrators' going unpunished because Rumsfeld or others seemed to bias the investigation. The Pentagon was forced to be circumspect in its comments and actions.

Getting "all" the information—good and bad—on the table was difficult because of the many people involved. There had been thousands of detainees under the control of hundreds of U.S. servicemembers. Done right—which meant thoroughly—information gathering would be difficult. Dribbling information out can be frustrating, especially when you want to release a flood, and you want the situation over. Missing something could be far worse.

The Pentagon did have more shocking photos of abuse in Abu Ghraib, ones that weren't seen in every newspaper and on every news program. In an effort to be more forthcoming, they allowed Congress to view them. Many made the case that those additional photos should be released in the name of transparency and because "they're going to get out there anyway." Thanks to the power of the Internet and the explosion of digital cameras, nobody—even to this day—could say how many photos were out there or know how to access them all. Of the arguments against releasing those photos, the strongest were made by the military leadership on the ground in Iraq. They made a passionate and convincing case that more photos released could inflame Iraqi public opinion against our troops more, putting them at even greater risk.

The nature of the crisis and the circumstances under which it occurred made the basic rules of communication far more difficult. Tell the story before someone else does, get all the facts out, answer all the questions. But the bottom line, no matter what facts were out there or what communications strategies were employed, was that this scandal was what it was: awful. And one person had the guts to talk about it that way.

Lost in most of the coverage of the prisoner scandal was something remarkable, something that transcends communications principles or tactics. And it relates to basic decency and honor. It will take years to appreciate, but Rumsfeld's testimony before the Senate Armed Services Committee on May 7, 2004, should be studied—and admired—as a true act of responsibility, accountability, and courage.

"In recent days, there has been a good deal of discussion about who bears responsibility for the terrible activities that took place at Abu Ghraib," Rumsfeld said in his opening statement before a packed committee room. "These events occurred on my watch. As secretary of defense, I am accountable for them. I take full responsibility. It is my obligation to evaluate what happened, to make sure those who have committed wrongdoing are brought to justice, and to make changes as needed to see that it doesn't happen again.

"I feel terrible about what happened to the Iraqi detainees. They are human beings. They were in U.S. custody. Our country had an obligation to treat them right. We didn't do that. That was wrong.

"To those Iraqis who were mistreated by members of U.S. armed forces, I offer my deepest apology. It was un-American. And it was inconsistent with the values of our nation."

Rumsfeld then spent several hours before the Senate and the House going into as much detail as he could in addressing the members' questions, comments, and accusations about what had happened. Most importantly, Rumsfeld did what very few people in leadership positions do in times of trouble. He took responsibility. He admitted mistakes. He apologized. He vowed to prevent future abuses and made clear his plan to do just that. He also offered his resignation to President Bush—twice.

It has become a cliché of business management books to quote Harry Truman's old adage that "the buck stops here." Scores of policy makers and executives have cheesy reproductions of the sign on their desks, as if to say, "I am responsible." Donald Rumsfeld doesn't need signs.

CHAPTER 2

Flood the Zone

---

*Transparency makes good things shine
and bad ones go away.*

T he motorcade carrying the secretary of defense pulled
up to a massive metal structure—a temporary building
about twenty football fields in size, housing about a
thousand military personnel rushing back and forth in desert
camouflage fatigues, a bustling city within the city of Doha,
Qatar, the headquarters for a possible invasion of Iraq. It was
December 2002. The United States was still pursuing diplomatic avenues, still prodding Saddam Hussein to provide credible evidence that he had complied with repeated demands by

the United Nations that he disarm. But we were running out of options, and Saddam was running out of tricks.

Rumsfeld and a small group of aides from the Pentagon were escorted to a modest trailer inside the building, where they filed into a cramped office. General Tommy Franks, head of U.S. Central Command, rose at the center of the room and began briefing Rumsfeld on his plans, carefully divided into four segments: an update on preconflict preparation; the initial stages of combat, if the president ordered it; major combat operations; and the aftermath.

The demeanor in the room was serious, businesslike, just-the-facts. True to form, Rumsfeld peppered Franks with questions. What if X happens? he would ask. If A and B don't work, what's plan C? And what about D? Franks reviewed targets for attack. Each one had been carefully vetted to minimize collateral damage to civilians, even if doing so placed our troops at risk by forgoing tactical surprise. Some collateral damage, of course, was inevitable.

"We know they're going to blame things on us that don't even occur, and we know they're going to exploit what does happen," Rumsfeld said.

"We're working on that," I said, "a communications plan that takes that into account."

My presence in the room was a deliberate signal by Rumsfeld that communications would be a top priority should hostilities occur—not as a public relations imperative but as a military one. Rumsfeld was one of the few people who instinctively understood how the Information Age had changed military conflict forever. Saddam was the mother of all liars. His propaganda machine—which would shape world opinion, especially the vaunted "Arab street"—would affect our ability to hold the coalition together, especially strategically critical allies in the Middle East. During operations in Afghanistan, Taliban fighters who appeared to be loosely organized had nonetheless managed to flash falsified photos around the Internet claiming we had struck civilian targets like hospitals. Saddam's operation was far more extensive, and we were concerned about its potential impacts. The world's understanding of the war would affect our ability to win it.

For months, communications planners had met with the war planners at every stage. Chairman of the Joint Chiefs, General Richard B. Myers, ensured this happened. He knew what the secretary knew: communications was central to war planning. Before the conflict began, we preempted Saddam's inevitable lies by reminding people of his past use of propaganda. In the event of combat, we had a communications plan ready for each target in advance—explaining its necessity and precisely how the attack had been planned to minimize collateral damage. Communications plans were in place for each stage of the war plan. My job now was to provide a high-level overview for the senior commanders.

"The essence of the communications plan is to flood the zone with information," I explained, "information dominance." The communications plan was nearly as exhaustive as the war plan, and its centerpiece was the embedding of journalists with military units on a scale never seen before. Embedding, an awkward name for an extraordinary effort by many people, had been in the works for months. There is nothing new about having journalists with the military; that has gone on for years. Reporters were accompanying U.S. and coalition forces in

Afghanistan or covering that conflict on their own as we began planning for Iraq.

Different times require different tactics, however, and we contemplated something for Iraq on a scale and scope that made it quantitatively and qualitatively different. One thing was certain: if we went to war with Iraq, the conflict would be very different from the Persian Gulf War in 1991. For starters, there would be no stopping at Kuwait this time; the goal would be to end the Hussein regime. More practically, the news media's technology had advanced dramatically, making transmission of product a lot easier under the right circumstances.

"Forget what you remember about the Persian Gulf War," we said repeatedly to the news media in the fall and winter of 2002. "If we go to war with Iraq, it will be dramatically different, and we need to plan for your coverage of such a conflict in dramatically different ways." Some got it. A lot didn't. It is hard to get people to move away from their frame of reference, no matter how hard you try.

We had several reasons for wanting massive embedding in Iraq. First of all, it was the right thing to do. Even before 9/11 and certainly after, Secretary Rumsfeld and most of the Pentagon's senior leadership shared one of my most strongly held beliefs: the American people deserve to know as much as possible about their military. What its objectives are, how it's performing—the good, the bad, and the ugly. I know how busted most people are for time in their daily lives. It's understandable that they neither know nor care much about many aspects of government. If there's one aspect of their government that they should care about, though, it's the military. And we did everything possible to make their military accessible to them.

Strategically, embedding reflected our confidence in three essential facts. First, we had a good story to tell—that our troops were topflight professionals taking great care to achieve their military objective while minimizing the impact on, and reaching out to help, civilians. Media coverage of that story would be the best antidote to Saddam's propaganda. Second, to the extent problems should occur, transparency—in other words, accountability—was the best guarantor that they would be fixed quickly. Third, when we just plain made mistakes—which was inevitable—the only way to maintain our credibility was to own up to them quickly.

In October of 2002, the public affairs team at the Pentagon held one of our regular meetings with media bureau chiefs. Topic A (and B and C) was a potential war with Iraq and our embedding plans for it. Rumsfeld dropped by at my request. I knew the bureau chiefs would grill him on the same topic, and it was important for him to put his personal seal on the program. After stressing firmly that any conversations about a conflict with Iraq at that time were purely hypothetical, the secretary talked about the desirability of having reporters witness the conflict. I could see some eyebrows rise and felt the skepticism in the room.

"Can you talk about the word 'desirability'?" one bureau chief asked. "Is that a core principle for you?"

"I think that as a principle, given our Constitution and the way our free system works, that it's always helpful, generally almost always helpful to have the press there to see things and be able to report and comment and provide information about what's taking place," Rumsfeld responded. "Is it a core principle? Sure."

One of the original sponsors of the Freedom of Information Act, Rumsfeld didn't just talk the talk when it came to access for the media and the public. He walked it. By the spring of 2002, Rumsfeld had already conducted more briefings, interviews, and outreach meetings than three of his predecessors put together. He and Chairman of the Joint Chiefs General Myers would regularly spend thirty to sixty minutes once or twice a week before the Pentagon press corps. At times of major activity, like the fall of '01 and the spring of '03, their appearances were more frequent. The purpose? Communicate as consistently and clearly as possible to the American people and publics worldwide on significant national security issues and events.

Rumsfeld's briefings became legendary, and with good reason. Blessed by *not* having lived in Washington for twenty-five years before returning for his second tour as defense secretary, Rumsfeld actually speaks clearly and concisely. He calls things like he sees them, and he divides information into the three categories prescribed by one of the best of Rumsfeld's Rules: "I know and will tell you. I know and I can't tell you. I don't know." Pretty simple yet highly effective guidelines for anybody dealing with the media, and especially good for people dealing with life-and-death matters on a daily basis. (Rumsfeld, by the way, credits CBS newsman Dan Rather for that rule.)

Thanks to 24/7 cable networks and intense interest in the military from September 11 on, many of the Pentagon press briefings were carried live and became "must see" TV. Most of the people watching loved Rumsfeld's blunt style, a view not shared by some of the media. State the facts wrong in your question? He'd cut you off at the knees. Base your query on unnamed sources quoted in the morning's papers? He might question why you couldn't go out and rustle up your own sources and find somebody willing to speak on the record. It's one thing to make a mistake. It's quite another to have them pointed out by an imposing secretary of defense on live television.

After a few months covering a SecDef who gave as good as he got, a handful of regular Pentagon correspondents confided to me their belief that the level of their work—at least that conducted in the briefing room—had gone up because of Rumsfeld's insistence on precision and accuracy. Okay, they had consumed more than a few beers at the time on a foreign trip, but they did say it.

For some, the standards were too demanding. One Knight Ridder reporter, not a Pentagon regular, made the mistake of strongly insinuating the answer—the wrong answer—in a question posed to Rumsfeld. The secretary paused, peered down at the reporter, and laced him.

"First of all, you're beginning with an illogical premise and proceeding perfectly logically to an illogical conclusion," Rumsfeld said, "which is a dangerous thing to do." We didn't see that reporter in the briefing room for several months.

Rumsfeld's critics—and trust me, I know there are some—say his language can be obtuse and deliberately misleading. Maybe it's like one of those whistles that only dogs can hear, but I understood the mission and intent of his words every time. A cottage industry grew out of efforts to decipher the "hidden meaning" behind one of Rumsfeld's oft-stated answers to queries about U.S. intelligence capabilities. "There are *known* knowns," he'd say. "And there are the known *unknowns,* and then there are the *unknown unknowns.*" To me it was simple. We understand some things, we don't understand others, and there are problems the existence of which we remain unaware.

I learned a lot watching Rumsfeld's briefings and became more comfortable at the podium as month after month of intense military action demanded a constant presence in the briefing room, scores of interviews and radio shows. I never enjoyed it, though, as my demeanor showed. I carefully avoided overreaction to the number of comments about me in stories that started out with "Despite her schoolmarm appearance, Clarke . . ." Better a schoolmarm than a segment on Comedy Central, I always thought to myself, intensely aware of the impact of every word, at home and abroad.

One *New York Times* story referred to me as "flintier" than Secretary Rumsfeld, prompting a very senior (and nice) military official to stop me in the hallway and say, "I'm not positive, but I think that's *New York Times* code for 'bitchier.'" Once called "the Gidget of politics" by columnist Bob Novak during the ill-fated Bush-Quayle campaign in 1992, I'd take "flintier" any day.

"Flinty" must be in the genetic makeup of the *Times*. The word came up again in a story announcing my departure from the Pentagon and expressing a not unheard of criticism that I was in the tank for Rumsfeld. "Ms. Clarke also grew fierce in her defense of Mr. Rumsfeld," Thom Shanker wrote, "revealing a flint-and-steely side to any correspondent she believed misrepresented the defense secretary's views or unfairly criticized her boss or the department." In the tank for Rumsfeld? Guilty.

The truth is, I didn't have to worry that much about Rumsfeld's views being misrepresented. That was because of a less noticed but—in the long term—just as important for transparency's sake practice of recording all senior officials' interviews and public events, transcribing them, and then posting the complete transcripts on Defenselink.mil, DOD's main Web site. A reporter would interview Rumsfeld, for example, and we would tape and transcribe the entire conversation. Once the reporter's piece appeared in print or was aired, we would post the entire transcript—questions and all—for everyone to see. We did it for two reasons. First, we wanted as much information as possible out there for the news media, Congress, and the general public to see. Given the complexity of issues with which we dealt, it was almost a guarantee that a newspaper or TV story could not give adequate space to many of our points. Second, we wanted to make sure quotes were not taken out of context.

When we first implemented the policy in early 2001, there was some grumbling. Most reporters, like most people, are resistant to change, and this was a change in their lives. Some objected, seeing it as an infringement or "taking" of their work. We did not accept interviews with those who would not agree to the guidelines: no hard feelings, we would explain, but those are the ground rules. We had more requests for interviews with the secretary and other senior Pentagon leadership than we could handle. Anybody who wanted to take himself off the list was OK by me. Few did, however, and some of the Pentagon regulars told me they not only supported the policy but thought it too had improved the overall quality of work.

But Iraq would require a level of transparency and unconventional thinking unseen at the Pentagon in years. As we headed into a potential war with Iraq, it was no secret that public opinion was not nearly as strong as it had been when we went into Afghanistan. You cannot have successful ongoing military operations without public support. I knew from personal experience that the more people saw of these incredible kids in uniform, the more they would support them. The discipline, bravery, and spirit of the men and women in uniform is a powerful force.

Moreover, we had had extensive experience the year before with Taliban propaganda. On one occasion, after we hit a military target in Kabul, Taliban forces ran to a nearby hospital and started moving patients to the bomb site to make it look like we had obliterated a hospital. Saddam, the mother of all liars, was apt to be far worse. The truth was on our side, and I wanted reporters all over the place so that they—and the reading and viewing public—knew it. Saddam's regime also had a well deserved reputation for war crimes, such as dressing soldiers as civilians to draw enemy forces into ambushes, and any such incidents would be much more credibly received around the world if they were reported by independent journalists in the field rather than asserted from a podium back in Washington. As Rumsfeld put it in the October 2002 bureau chief meeting, "It's helpful to the extent you have people who are journalists and are accurate and professional with you that can see those things on the ground when they happen."

Perhaps most important, embedding was a military strategy in addition to a public affairs one. We had to keep other Middle Eastern regimes out of the conflict. If false propaganda about American forces took hold, the so-called Arab street—public opinion in the Arab world—might erupt. Regimes might well be overthrown, and other countries could be drawn into the war. Here as always, transparency was our best defense, so we embedded many journalists from international media outlets like Agence France-Presse and Al Jazeera as well as American reporters.

Despite our constant admonition that a twenty-first-century war with Iraq would be far different from anything seen before, we did learn some important lessons from the Persian Gulf War in 1991. In the many conversations we had with journalists who had covered that conflict and bureau chiefs who had tried to manage the flow of news, we heard the same thing again and again. In 1991 reporters were allowed out with military units, they said, but the military severely restricted what they could report, and even when they were allowed to report, the logistics of getting their stories back home often made it impossible to do so. If we were to succeed in these new, unconventional, post-9/11 times, we would need a very different military mission and intent.

Our position was communicated in operational guidelines put out by Central Command in February of 2003 to military units with whom reporters would be embedded.

> We need to tell the factual story—good or bad—before others seed the media with disinformation and distortions, as they most certainly will continue to do. Our people in the field need to tell our story. . . . These ground rules recognize the right of the media to cover military operations and are in no way intended to prevent release of derogatory, embarrassing, negative or uncomplimentary information.

Our team decided to shoot for as broad and deep an embedding program as we could, assuming it would probably get cut in half anyway. Bryan Whitman, my deputy and our point man on the project, started working in late 2002 with the military services on how many slots they could give us for embedded reporters. Bryan, a former Special Forces soldier with an impressive military record, has excellent public affairs skills and an insatiable appetite for work. Dropping by my office ten to fifteen times on a slow day, Bryan would report in regularly on what the services were coughing up. "Thirty-five so far from the Navy," he'd rattle off, "twenty from the Air Force and Marines, and twenty from the Army. " Not bad, but not what we wanted.

It was not lost on Bryan, me, or anyone else that the Army would have the largest number of forces in any war. They could and should easily accommodate a lot more reporters. Playing to the power of competition, we decided to let each service know, quietly, what the others were ponying up. It couldn't hurt to play off their institutional rivalries. It worked. Whitman thought as many as 250 reporters might eventually head into battle. In the end, we embedded over 700, and we could have accommodated more, had news organizations had enough correspondents to fill the slots.

The program required thorough planning, to say the least. There were the logistics of reporters' getting their stories from the field to their home news organizations. We wanted them to be able to use their own equipment if they wanted to, but to have ours available just in case. We also decided early on not to assign individual reporters to specific units. Doing so would have opened us to charges of media manipulation or favoritism. Instead, we allotted slots to news organizations, and they made assignments.

The closer we got to what became the start of the war, the more those involved—our Pentagon team, many correspondents, and their bureau chiefs—started to believe that we might just be able to pull it off. We were going to produce very different coverage of military combat.

Many people in the Pentagon and the White House were nervous, and for good reason. The biggest section in the briefing deck that we used to get buy-in was "Things That Can Go Wrong," starting with "Journalists get killed and captured." Both happened, sadly. If the media revealed a unit's locations or plans, people might get killed or a mission might fail. We worked with numerous bureau chiefs and correspondents on a clear and simple rule: don't reveal information that could put the success of the mission or lives at risk. That was a guideline that the media could and did embrace. If reporters or photographers violated it, they could be expelled from their unit.

But by the time I briefed our commanders in Qatar that December, they were on board. Many times since, I've been asked how I convinced them to go along with embedding. The truth is that I never had to. There was some institutional resistance in the Pentagon, as well as some valid concerns. But the senior officials and commanders—from Rumsfeld, Myers, and Franks on down—got it from the beginning. Rumsfeld didn't just go along. He was a strong backer of the embedding program who instinctively understood that transparency was on our side.

On March 17, Rumsfeld, his special assistant Larry Di Rita, and I watched in the secretary's office as President Bush addressed the nation from the Oval Office. The president's tone was grave, his expression solemn. "All the decades of deceit and cruelty have now reached an end. Saddam Hussein and his sons must leave Iraq within forty-eight hours. Their refusal to do so will result in military conflict, commenced at a time of our choosing."

I felt resigned. There seemed to be few realistic options for avoiding conflict. Still, I was grasping for shimmers of hope. "I really wonder what kind of impact this is having," I said. "Could it force Saddam to cave?"

"It would be a wonderful thing, wouldn't it?" Rumsfeld replied quietly. Opponents of the war later caricatured Rumsfeld as a hawk eager to take up arms. He believes in a strong, forward-leaning national defense, but he takes no joy in war. He has simply seen too much. He knows too many people who have been hurt or killed. As SecDef, he has spent too many weekends at Walter Reed Army Medical Center visiting wounded soldiers. He is willing to go to war, but only as the last conceivable resort.

The atmosphere amid the Pentagon leadership was remarkably calm. The war plan was in place, and the embedding program was ready to go. Two days after the president delivered his forty-eight-hour ultimatum, American intelligence got a reliable report that Saddam and his sons were hiding out in a house in suburban Baghdad. If we struck immediately, there was a chance—albeit a slim one—the entire war might be averted. Rumsfeld called to fill me in, describing the strike under consideration in general terms.

"If we do this, how would you handle it?" he asked.

"I'd be as transparent as we can be without putting our planes at risk. As soon as they're out of harm's way, we need to acknowledge the attack." Embedded media were already on the ground anyway. Many news organizations had their own "unilateral" correspondents in Baghdad—reporters who were covering the situation on their own. They would know about the attack almost as soon as it occurred. And there was no reason to be reticent about targeting Saddam personally. Attacks on an enemy's command-and-control structure are an accepted part of warfare.

Many senior Pentagon officials left at a reasonable hour—around eight p.m.—that night, half hoping we could avoid arousing suspicion among the media in the building that an attack was imminent. The Pentagon has legendary "spider senses," and the building was already buzzing with speculation. Several of the correspondents, I am sure, had figured out that something was up. I got home, put the kids to bed, turned on the TV, and started flipping around among the cable news channels. I switched the channel about a dozen times in rapid-fire succession before my husband, Brian, boiled over in good-natured irritation.

"Goddamnit, give me that," he blurted out, grabbing the remote control. Brian had no idea an attack was coming. The information was classified, obviously. It would have been illegal, not to mention highly improper, for me to tell him. He and I had a clear understanding that Brian always respected. I doubt he especially wanted to know any of the Pentagon's secrets anyway. All he knew was that whatever was on ESPN—or any other channel, for that matter—was bound to be better than watching me and my short attention span flip among news networks.

The attack occurred late that night. The next morning, ground forces began pouring over the border into Iraq, stunning an already disorganized Iraqi military that had expected weeks of air attacks first. I spent the bulk of the next day checking in with mid- and senior-level military officials, from the Pentagon to Central Command headquarters in Qatar, to see how embedding was working out. As the day wore on, word came back that problems were popping up—assessments being reported that shouldn't have been, units whose positions were being revealed, and so forth—and that General Tommy Franks, commander of the operation, was ready to pull the plug on the whole embedding program.

I pondered whether to intervene with Franks. He had the lives of thousands of people in his hands, and he was in the opening hours of a war. Who was I to be harassing him with more problems? But I decided embedding was too important from both a military and a communications perspective. I had to try to preserve it. Near midnight, I picked up the secure line at my house and asked Cables, the Pentagon's communications staff, to connect me with General Franks in Qatar. I had to shout to be heard.

"General," I began, "I hear we've got some problems."

"Goddamn right we do," he snapped.

I was just beginning to make my case for embedding—assuring Franks we would correct the problems and that we had procedures in place for doing so—when the line dropped. I called back and got a staff officer who, no doubt, had borne the brunt of the pressure-cooker environment in which Franks was naturally caught at that moment.

"You want to talk to him *again*, ma'am?" he stammered. I did. With Franks back on the phone, I started making my case once more when the line dropped again. Meanwhile, Charlie, my three-year-old, wandered out of his room. "Mom, you're *talking* too loud," he complained.

We lost the connection several more times before Franks and I got through the conversation. To his lasting credit, he recognized the importance of the program and took the time to hear me out. Franks let out a palpable sigh.

"All right," he said. "You've clearly thought this through." The embedding program could go forward.

I would "see" Franks the next morning via the secure video conference that we held every morning to brief Rumsfeld and his top aides. I was nervous about what Franks might do, understanding completely that he was probably still furious with me. I had to do something, I thought, to break the ice.

I had my staff make a sign that said I LOVE GENERAL FRANKS! Some tough guy in uniform who helped make the sign added a lovely stencil of a cupid with a bow and arrow. As the videoconference started, Franks saw Rumsfeld in his chair and me, holding the sign over the SecDef's head.

Franks laughed. Briefly.

Initial bumps in the road notwithstanding, the overwhelming majority of embedded journalists acted professionally and responsibly throughout the conflict. We made more mistakes in the public affairs shop than they did in the field. Any number of them had access to information that would have made for a great story but which would have put troops at risk, and they almost never reported it. Their sense of responsibility was clear the first night. Several journalists were embedded aboard the aircraft carrier that served as the launching pad for our first strike on Saddam's compound. Our rules prevented them from announcing any attack on the air before it happened. Still, any one of them might have tried to report this one, if only by questioning activity on the carrier. Not a single one did until our planes were out of harm's way.

The volume and velocity of coverage surprised us all. "The first full day of television coverage of the invasion of Iraq revealed not the fog of war but a firestorm of amazing combat images," Alessandra Stanley wrote in the *New York Times* on March 21, 2003. "From Navy fighter jets roaring off the deck of the carrier *Constellation* to grainy, green night-scope glimpses of American tanks moving across the Kuwaiti border into Iraq, television showed more live military action in one day than in the entire 1991 war." Bureau chiefs went from worries that there would be little "product" coming back from the war to concerns about how to sift through the huge volumes being sent back by their correspondents.

The early reports from the news media were good (General Franks's justified heartburn notwithstanding). A *USA Today* editorial summed the situation up as early as March 27:

> On the home front, the biggest surprise came in how easily the public could follow the war's developments as they were occurring, thanks to the Pentagon's decision to "embed" reporters in the field. In an unprecedented arrangement, more than 500 reporters were invited to accompany troops on combat missions. In return, they agreed not to disclose the information deemed sensitive by the Pentagon. Vietnam was the first "living-room war." But Iraq is the first war reported to home audiences in real time.

A *New York Times* piece by David Carr in late March captured the always-present concern that embedded reporters might be co-opted by the troops they covered while acknowledging the dramatically different coverage:

> A new standard of openness and immediacy has been created for war coverage, raising the question of whether

reporters, soldiers, or news consumers will ever be satisfied with less. The reporters say that they can be objective in their coverage, but that their ability to remain detached is being tested every day by this new level of engagement.

According to Hampton Sides in the March 24, 2003, *New Yorker,* although skepticism ran high among many prior to the start of the war, "It remained to be seen how much latitude would be afforded the media once the bullets began flying, but by the look of things the Pentagon truly wanted us to be right there on the battlefield, free and unfettered, reporting precisely what we saw."

There are always critics; embedding had some then and still does today. Most were concerned that embedded reporters might become biased toward the U.S. military. Analysis is subjective, of course, but I saw little evidence of that happening.

All you have to do is look at the coverage then—print or electronic—and you'll see that the first couple of months produced primarily factual, straight reporting. The huge volume of material coming back from embedded reporters, and the ease with which many of them could transmit live, meant straight reporting dominated the news coverage. Not "analysis" or talking heads back in Washington helping networks fill time, just straightforward hard reporting.

"You know the expression 'unplugged'?" I asked CBS correspondent Steve Kroft in an April, 2003, *60 Minutes* interview about embedding and the first major military conflict of the Information Age. "This is the U.S. military unplugged. We have close to seven hundred independent, objective, tough-nosed, hardscrabble journalists out there of all sizes and shapes, and they're showing it like it's happening. It's live. You're watching this war live. . . . How much more of a nonspin zone could you have than that?"

More important than any assessment by us in Washington or ivory towers was the fact that the overwhelming majority of reporters gutsy enough to be embedded praised how things worked. Glenn Garvin of the *Miami Herald* wrote a piece called "New allies on Front Line: the Media, the Military," in which he examined the pros and cons of embedding. "That's not to say that the reports from the embedded reporters are false or that they're under the influence of military spinmasters," he wrote on March 27, 2003. "'Battlefield commanders don't have time to spin,'" he quoted veteran combat correspondent Walt Rogers saying as the CNN correspondent traveled with the reconnaissance unit of the Third Infantry Division. "'There's no public affairs officer here. The lieutenant colonel in command of this unit tells us the good and the bad, and we can see it in his face when the news is going to be bad.'"

A *Dallas Morning News* story by Doug J. Swanson on March 23, 2003, underscored just how close the journalists were to real combat:

Jim Landers, a Washington-based reporter for the *Dallas Morning News,* was with the First Marine Division when it led the ground invasion of Iraq on Thursday. He said he and other journalists were able to witness combat. "We were in the back of an amphibious armored vehicle, a couple hundred yards behind a wall of tanks fighting their way across Iraq," he said. "We could see the muzzle flashes. We had people shooting at us. We had artillery landing around us."

He and other journalists used satellite telephones to report the opening attack of the ground war through the night.

"It was as if they had put journalists in the landing craft at D-Day, and we had been filing reports from the beach as it happened," he said. "When you have access like that, I don't know what more you want."

To a very large extent, embedding did achieve our objectives. A few days into the war, a front-page photo in the *New York Times* showed Iraqi soldiers dressed as civilians, a clear violation of the Geneva Conventions. Showing the photo to Secretary Rumsfeld, I said, "We could have said a thousand times that the Iraqi regime was dressing its soldiers as civilians to ambush coalition forces. Some people would have believed us; others wouldn't." It was a clear win to have the international news media report Saddam's atrocities.

Despite many dire predictions, the Arab street didn't erupt, and Saddam's propaganda operation was widely understood to be so absurd that even late-night comedians took to calling his spokesman, Mohammed Saeed al-Sahhaf, "Comical Ali." Many of al-Sahhaf's briefings were near-lunatic flights of fancy. But in the old days, many of his claims would have been reduced to he-said, she-said reports—Saddam's regime said thus-and-such, and American officials denied it—that would have placed him just on the edge of believability. Not with embedding. One day, the networks showed a split-screen shot that captured the power of embedding: On one side of the screen, al-Shahhaf was claiming the Iraqis had just defeated U.S. troops at the Baghdad airport. On the other, U.S. tanks were rolling into the city.

In ways and volume that far exceeded most expectations, the American people saw—often in stunning live coverage—the bravery and skill of our forces. It's one thing to watch a movie like *Saving Private Ryan* to appreciate the dangers and sacrifices of our military. It's something spectacularly different to see those dangers, that bravery, and know it's the real thing.

On one occasion, I stood in my kitchen listening to the radio as I prepared for my first call of the day at four a.m. Ted Koppel was delivering a report describing the actions of the unit with which he was embedded. I put down my coffee, ignored my notepad, just listened. It was riveting. Incredible, I thought. When was the last time anyone stood by a radio and—without the distraction of a workout, a commute, or some other daily chore—just *listened*?

Of course, it was my job to be interested in what our troops were doing. But embedding reached a lot deeper. In the early days of the war, I was walking in downtown Washington when I overheard two young women—dressed more like Britney Spears wannabes than military junkies—talking about what they had seen on TV the night before.

"Could you believe what the First MEF did yesterday?" the one woman said to the other, talking about the Marine Expeditionary Force hauling its way north to Baghdad at an incredible pace. Agree or disagree with the decision to go to war, the embedding made clear to many people that our troops deserve our appreciation and support.

Around the same time, I went up to Capitol Hill for one of the frequent briefings Pentagon officials gave to keep members and their staff informed. Always prepared, Colonel Rhynedance had me there a few minutes early, and I was gulping down what was probably my tenth coffee of the day. It was about noon. A woman came rushing up and grabbed my arm, making Rhynedance—who, unlike me, took his responsibility for my security seriously—unhappy. It turned out she was the mother of a serviceman in the 101st.

"Thank you so much for that embedding," she shouted. "I think I saw my son last night on TV. I'm not positive, but I know I saw his friend Jeff, and they're always together, so it had to be him. It's so wonderful to be able to follow them on television. My friends and I have viewing parties every night to watch the war."

The coverage was riveting for many people, especially the families of the U.S. military over there doing the hard and very dangerous work. And not all of them were as enthusiastic as the woman who accosted me on Capitol Hill—with good reason. For those whose loved ones were injured or killed, the embedding brought it home to them in all too real a fashion.

Nancy Chamberlin, the mother of Marine Major Jay Aubin, who was killed in a helicopter crash, did a phone interview with Tom Brokaw on NBC on March 21 in which she expressed her dismay with the images being sent home every day. "I truly admire what all of the network news and all the new technology is doing today to bring it into our homes," she said, "but for the mothers and the wives who are out there watching, it is murder. It's—it's heartbreak. We can't leave the television. And I just need you to be aware that technology is—it's great. But there are moms, there are dads, there are wives out there that are suffering because of this."

As devastating as those images could be for some people— and my heart breaks for them and their loss—I still know that embedding was the right thing to do. Everything about embedding was truthful—the good, the bad, and the in-between. And if as a society we are willing to ask young men and women to fight and die for us, then we should have the courage to recognize publicly their commitment and sacrifices.

As the *Columbus Dispatch* wrote in a March 25, 2003, editorial, "The United States is an open society, and coverage of its war should reflect that."

Exactly.

Even when bad things happened—and they always do in wars—having the spotlight of the news media helped. Early in the war, there was a terrible event when a van approached a Marine checkpoint near Najaf, about a hundred miles south of Baghdad, and ignored signs to stop. As the van approached, the Marines tried to wave it off and fired warning shots. The van kept coming. The Marines fired into the grille of the van, trying to disable it, and still the van came on. The Marines then did what they were trained and expected to do: they opened fire on the van, killing or injuring everyone inside. The van's occupants were civilians, including children.

It was awful for all the obvious reasons. Your heart breaks for the people killed and their families. The Marines were distraught at what had happened. But the coverage—there were several correspondents there—was accurate and comprehensive, and it provided a context that wouldn't have been there if they hadn't been on the scene when the tragedy occurred. Flooding the zone works. When something goes well, people see and hear it. When something goes badly, it's dealt with directly and quickly.

Even better, flooding the zone can prevent problems from occurring. The majority of our troops are both trained professionals and very decent people, so not many of them needed accountability from the media to keep them on the straight and narrow. But knowing a camera is perched over your shoulder at any given moment is also a pretty powerful incentive to do the right thing. Almost a year after I left the Pentagon, when the story of prisoner abuse at Abu Ghraib prison broke, a former colleague (one never enthusiastic about embedding) wise-cracked, "I bet you wouldn't have wanted any reporters embed-ded at Abu Ghraib."

"I absolutely would have," I snapped back. "If that prison had been crawling with reporters, this never would have hap-pened." Embedding was real-time accountability, faster, stronger, and more visible than any court-martial or congressional inves-tigation.

Flooding the zone can work in the private sector too. Every time I make that point, someone from the corporate world tells me I don't understand, that large-scale transparency would never work in the private sector, that government and business are different creatures. Yeah, I respond, they are. Military com-manders hold people's lives in their hands. If anyone has a ready-made excuse for retreating behind a wall of secrecy, they do. And if they can let the sunshine in, anyone can.

For businesses, that doesn't mean embedding a reporter in every cubicle or opening every board meeting to the media—although you might want to consider more of that than you'd initially think. What it does mean is flooding the zone with every bit of information you can. And make that information com-prehensible to the average man in the street, not so complex it requires a team of lawyers to decipher it.

Better yet, if you really want to reach all the way down the totem pole of human intelligence, make it comprehensible to me. When you study the safety of your products, release everything you find in language the people who actually use them can understand. "If I can understand it," I have told countless clients, bosses, and colleagues over the years as I pushed them to explain themselves, "anyone can."

Now, some corollaries apply here. We'll get back to these in more detail in subsequent chapters, but keep them in mind for now.

First off, flooding the zone is an expression of confidence in your product and your people. If you've got a pig, don't expect the media to apply the lipstick for you out of sheer gratitude that you opened your doors to them. Their job is to hold you accountable. It's *your* job to have a good story to tell. Moreover, when you flood the zone, the media are, so to speak, only one of the floodgates. You need to use every tactic, every communications vehicle, at your disposal—from cyberspace to speeches to the secretaries who answer the phones.

Please, please, please, when you're getting information out there, *get it right*. Flood the zone with *accurate* information, not just whatever reports come across your desk. On a day like September 11, or in the middle of a war in which journalists are clamoring for every scrap of information, that takes tremendous discipline. And getting it right includes flooding the zone with negative information as well as positive news. Once you endorse transparency as a standard, you get the benefit of credibility. You also get the responsibility of airing all your laundry. The first time you withhold a single nugget of information for fear that you'll look bad, you forfeit every bit of credibility you've gained—and probably erode what you had before.

Last—and, trust me, not least—if you're going to flood the zone, flood the zone. A trickle won't do it—a lesson I learned the hard way early in the war on terror.

In January 2002, we started holding detainees from the hostilities in Afghanistan at the U.S. naval base in Guantánamo Bay, Cuba—GITMO, in military parlance. Anything new is hard for most people, and GITMO was very new. Enormous decisions loomed. In a typical war, you repatriate prisoners after the enemy has surrendered. But many of these prisoners weren't loyal to any particular country, and many of them had declared permanent war against the United States. Were they lawful combatants, or unlawful? Were they protected by the Geneva Conventions? What kind of legal representation were they entitled to? With the base about four hundred miles from Miami, Florida, were there security concerns? What would the detainees' facilities be like?

The interest from the press was understandable and intense. They wanted every detail of every aspect—transport, clothing, interrogations, toilet facilities. Human rights organizations expressed concerns about the detainees' treatment before any of them had been flown to GITMO.

I think some concern was genuine. I think some—especially much of the concern expressed by foreigners—was designed to appease their domestic critics. I know too many people in the United States—including me—get their basic legal understanding from watching reruns of *Law and Order*, so few could fathom the entirely different legal situation in which we found ourselves a few short months after 9/11. Even fewer could imagine that, perhaps, we needed a new way of dealing with combatants in the most unconventional of wars. These detainees were not car thieves or even combatants in World War II. The typical rules of war—the enemy surrenders, and you send their soldiers home—didn't apply. To start with, the enemy wasn't a country. It wasn't even a defined geographical area. And regardless, they weren't going to surrender.

In my experience, the majority of the time the detainees received good treatment. Even though lawyers concluded that al Qaeda operatives were not lawful combatants and thus were not protected by the Geneva Conventions, Rumsfeld, the president, and others made it very clear—repeatedly—that the detainees were to be treated in accordance with the principles of the conventions.

Within days of the first detainees' arrival at GITMO, we did our best to make sure the world knew that. We briefed Congress and others in the administration. We briefed friends and allies at home and abroad. We used the Pentagon press briefings:

January 14, 2002
Assistant Secretary of Defense Victoria Clarke: As of today, there are four hundred fourteen detainees in Afghanistan; there are twenty in Guantánamo. And there have been a lot of questions, obviously, about the treatment of detainees. So I just wanted to give you—share with you a few of the details of what is going on there. Each day the detainees are given three culturally appropriate meals. They have daily opportunities to shower, exercise, and receive medical attention.

Clearly, that didn't feed the appetite. There were more questions later in the briefing, and people wanted what we weren't giving them—access to the facilities, an "up close and personal" look, if you will, at the detainees and their situation.

My instinct was to open the place up. Let the cameras into GITMO so everyone—from our foreign critics to human rights organizations to everyday Americans who were legitimately concerned about what was happening there—could see what was happening. We had nothing to hide; on the contrary, we had a good story to tell: we were treating detainees well.

The challenge was that the Geneva Conventions specifically prohibit holding detainees up to public ridicule or humiliation. Over the years, lawyers had interpreted that requirement to mean that media could have no access to the detainees; access might be considered humiliating or embarrassing. Very specifically, it meant detainees could not be photographed at all. I argued the opposite: that allowing the media in would both prove that we were abiding by the conventions and provide a means of accountability to ensure we did.

With lawyers pulling me in one direction and my communications instincts tugging in another, I chose the worst possible path: rather than flooding the zone, we let a little bit of information out. After long, frustrating, and mostly losing negotiations with lawyers and base officials, we did get media to GITMO, but there were tight restrictions on their distance from the detainees' cells—about 150 yards—and on what kind of images they could obtain: none, for example, in which the detainees' faces could be seen.

We got permission to release select DOD photos of some of the detainees. Not ideal in my book, certainly, but better than nothing, I thought. The pressure from the media was unbearable. Mark this down: that's never a good reason to do anything.

I felt that releasing select images could allay some of our critics. Boy, was I wrong. And did I ever misread what was in those photos.

With a few years' distance and Abu Ghraib in the rearview mirror, the reaction to those first images—detainees in orange jumpsuits, kneeling near a wire fence as they were processed into the facility—seems almost silly. But the reaction at the time wasn't. The reaction at the time was anything but amusing. It was—to employ an overused word—a firestorm. A worldwide, front-page, several-day firestorm. Instead of showing the care and concern with which we treated the detainees, the photos served as high-octane fuel for our critics and doubters. "Torture" ran across the top of lots of foreign tabloids. "Images Raise Concern over Detainee Treatment," blasted others.

It was an awful and absolute misrepresentation of reality, and it was my fault. The problem wasn't that we released too much, it was that we explained too little. We just released the photos with brief descriptions and left it at that. What they really needed were long, exhaustive, detailed captions and probably, in hindsight, a full briefing describing the circumstances. In some of the photos, for example, the detainees were wearing noise-reducing headphones. Some critics called that "sensory deprivation." Actually, it was a safety measure—they had just been flown over on some very loud airplanes—but we never bothered to explain that. The detainees were forced to kneel while they were handcuffed and processed. We didn't explain that either, which allowed other critics to say we were forcing the detainees into poses of subjugation. They were wearing surgical masks. That was to prevent the spread of tuberculosis, but again, we were silent, and—for reasons I really don't get—the critics latched on to that too.

I was the one who blew it, but in the Pentagon press briefing on January 22, 2002, Rumsfeld took the heat.

Q: Mr. Secretary, since you want to clear the air about the detainees, one of the things that seems to have aroused public opinion and the parliamentarians from Britain was this photograph that was released that showed the detainees kneeling with their hands bound behind their backs.

Rumsfeld: That's right. Yeah.

Q: Could you just explain what that photograph—

Rumsfeld: I will, to the best of my ability. It's probably unfortunate that it was released. It's the tension between wanting to meet the desires of the press to know more and the public to know more.

Rumsfeld went on to detail how detainees came into the facility and the precautions we took for everyone's safety, including theirs. His five-minute "caption" and explanation gave much more information and put in context what was sadly lacking in the hastily released photos.

Later in the same briefing:

Q: Mr. Secretary, you said it was unfortunate that that photograph was released. I would just argue that it was unfortunate that it wasn't released with more information.

Rumsfeld: Maybe. Yeah. That's fair.

Q: The lesson here ought not to be—

Rumsfeld: I mean, I'm not blaming anyone for not releasing it, but—

Q: —less information or withholding photographs, but simply releasing more information—

Rumsfeld: Fair enough.

Q: —so we can make better judgments.

Q: And Mr. Secretary, would it be more beneficial to provide more open access to the media to allow the media to see for itself how these prisoners are being treated, to convey that information? You've spent now nearly an hour trying to explain what's going on there, when over the past couple of weeks, if the media would've had more open access, the stories that you're telling today would have been, perhaps, better told over the past couple of weeks.

Rumsfeld continued the exchange over access for another ten minutes, time that would have been better spent on other topics. Note, by the way, that Rumsfeld never blamed me for releasing the photos even though everyone in the room knew I was responsible, not to mention the fact that he would have been completely justified in giving me a public kick in the pants. Rumsfeld happens to be a stand-up guy who doesn't sell people out.

The International Committee of the Red Cross (ICRC) visited the facility frequently but did not discuss with the media what they saw. So the best we could offer the skeptics, sincere and otherwise, was "Trust us, they're getting good treatment." We pushed the edge of the envelope as far as we could, incurring the wrath of lawyers and base commanders along the way. In late January, Rumsfeld traveled to GITMO with Senators Inouye, Stevens, Feinstein, and Hutchison. Despite just about everybody's objections, I insisted that we take media along. If we couldn't get the media inside the camp itself, I thought, at least we can have them close to people who did get in.

At a press briefing after they toured the facilities, the senators described generally what they had seen and all vouched for what they believed to be good treatment of the detainees. Senator Feinstein, a former head of California's Bureau of Prisons, remarked that the GITMO detainees lived better than some California inmates she had seen. "I'll be very candid with you," the *New York Post* quoted Senator Feinstein. "I would much rather be here in an 8 [feet] by 8 [feet] cell with a breeze than locked down in Folsom prison in California."

The Information Age is not for the fainthearted. To succeed, you have to be very forward-leaning. In good times, that means putting a bright and constant spotlight on your accomplishments. In bad times, it means focusing on the mistakes with the same aggressiveness, so they get cleaned up faster. If you're going to tell your own story, you have to really tell it. Especially when the topic is complex or controversial, half measures won't get you there. Give them the whole picture.

CHAPTER 3

Have More Than
One Weapon in Your Arsenal

*I don't think too many
seventeen-year-olds read the editorial
pages of the* Post-Gazette.

ew soldiers would go into battle with one weapon. You
shouldn't in communications warfare either. Communications professionals used to view their jobs as dealing
primarily with the media. That's still important, but the news
media alone are no longer the only, or always the most effective,
means of reaching your audiences. And you have to communicate on multiple channels, if only because the information envi-

ronment today is so chaotic, you can't assume any one vehicle will break through. Take what's typically viewed as advertising these days, and you begin to get a sense of the challenge you face in reaching and influencing people. Thirty years ago the average American was exposed to approximately six hundred messages a day. In 2005? Between three and five thousand.

Here's how the *Economist* captured the new information environment:

> It has been calculated that the average American is subjected to some 3,000 advertising messages every day. If you add in everything from the badges on cars to slogans on sweatshirts, the ads in newspapers, on taxis, in subways and even playing on TVs in the lifts, then some people could be exposed to more than that number just getting to the office.

And those assessments don't take into account the flood of e-mails—whether they're spam or welcome—instant messages, Web sites, blogs, and others, all of which are competing to fill the information vacuum. Factor them in, and it becomes crystal clear why a comprehensive communications program is critical to success in the information era.

Start with the obvious—working with the media. And I say "working with" because that's what you have to do to be successful. Whether you're the head of a multinational corporation or the manager of a small store in a three-thousand-person town, chances are you will encounter the media someday. More precisely, you should *want* to encounter them. Love them or hate them, the news media are not going away. And I happen to think they have important jobs to do.

I know four-star generals who have been in combat numerous times and received serious injuries. They've commanded thousands in battle and run major parts of the Department of Defense—the world's largest organization. Yet they would rather pull their fingernails off than deal with reporters. It's the same in corporate America. Most people—with the notable exception of the media hounds who probably *shouldn't* be seeking the spotlight—have a real aversion to dealing with the media.

Maybe a scant two years trying to be a photographer at the now-defunct *Washington Star* is what made the difference for me. I saw what reporters, editors, and photographers went through on a daily basis. I got a clear sense of the pressures they faced—demanding editors inside the newsroom, and everything from competition to physical risk on the outside. Shaky hands and bad eyes steered me away from a life as a photographer, but that experience did give me a sense of what it was like to walk in the media's shoes, an invaluable experience when it comes to working with anybody, particularly somebody who may have a different agenda.

And since you've paid good money for this book—or at least I hope you have—I'll let you in on a little trade secret. Just don't tell any of my fellow communications consultants that I spilled the beans. Telling you what I'm about to tell you is like breaking the magician's code.

OK, dim the lights. Pull the shades. Listen carefully.

Working with the media is not rocket science.

In fact, it's pretty straightforward.

When people became frustrated with the media, Joyce Rumsfeld captured the point perfectly: "Remember, they have their job to do, and you have yours." Excellent advice when you're trying to take the emotion out of a hot situation.

First of all, be responsive. That means you need to return calls and return them promptly. By the time a reporter calls you, chances are he's already getting bugged by his editor and feels under the gun.

In the early 1980s Pete Teeley was then Vice President Bush's press secretary in the first Reagan administration. Pete commanded respect and affection among the press, mostly because he understood their business and was a fierce but fair advocate for his boss. Trying to distract me while the rest of the staff planned a surprise going-away party before I left for Kansas and the ill-fated Morris Kay congressional campaign, Pete said, "Kid, I want to tell you a few things about this business. Return your calls—all of them . . . no matter how late you have to do it."

That was the extent of Pete's advice that day, but it was sound. Over twenty-five years later, I am still obsessed with returning calls—to everyone, not just the media. I may not always tell you what you want, but I will return your call. Once in a while, it's fine for an article to state that "so-and-so declined to comment." But "so-and-so did not return phone calls" is appalling. It's rude, and it's dumb. It irritates reporters, and it makes it look like you had something to hide, when the only thing that was hiding was the message on your desk. (I say this, I should add, knowing there are probably at least a few dozen people who did not get their calls returned by me. Nobody is perfect, especially me. I apologize.)

Second, be accurate with the news media. This rule goes above and beyond the obvious tenet to tell the truth. Don't quote a number unless you're sure about it. If you name a name, make sure you've got the right one. Don't expect a reporter to have the time or inclination to check your facts. Do the job yourself so you don't have to clean things up later. If you're not sure, say so. If you want a reporter to have some facts, don't guess.

You know how many press secretaries it takes to screw in a lightbulb, don't you? Can I get back to you on that? It is OK to say exactly that to a reporter, but then follow up—quickly. If you can be fast and accurate—and in most cases, you should be able to—do so. If the choice is between responding quickly and responding correctly, choose accuracy.

Finally, be truthful—totally, completely—even if all you're being truthful about is that you don't know or can't say. Say what you can say—honestly—and then go no further. Of course, in the national security arena, there are often operational security considerations that make category two the guiding force. In the business world, there sometimes is proprietary information that you'd rather not reveal to a competitor. That's fine. But there often *is* a great deal you can say. If you cannot talk about a specific product that you might launch next year, you certainly can explain your philosophy on how you decide what products are worth bringing to market.

In the early weeks of the Iraq war, the questions from the media were fast and furious—often very specific questions about the scope or timing of particular troop movements. For obvious reasons, we couldn't give that kind of information. But we could use the question to impart some information and do a little education at the same time. Major General Stanley A. McChrystal, Vice Director of Operations for the Joint Staff, was one of the briefers then, and one of the best ever at that approach.

March 29, 2003

> Q: *Do you have anything or does the general have anything*
> *on elements of the Second Armored Cavalry Regiment*
> *going ahead of schedule, or anything on additional*
> *forces going into the north?*

McChrystal could have just refused to answer the question on grounds of operational security. Instead, he used it as an opportunity to provide information on the regiment.

> *General McChrystal: The Second Light Armored Cavalry*
> *Regiment at Fort Polk, in fact, has been on orders. It's a*
> *Humvee-mounted cavalry element with aviation as*
> *well. There are discussions under way about potentially*
> *moving up a part of its force to an earlier deployment.*
> *I'm not aware of the specific time line at this point.*
> *Clarke: I'll have a general comment about the plan.*
> *Obviously it's up to General Franks to decide who moves*
> *where and at what pace. But the plan has always been*
> *built in such a way that it's scaleable. That probably*
> *isn't a real word, but it reflects the truth, which is a*
> *plan that is flexible and it can adjust up and down as*
> *needed. And that's what General Franks works with.*

Mrs. Moll, my third-grade teacher and a stickler on grammar, would be appalled, but you get the point: again, we're using a question we could have just refused to answer to discuss the philosophy of the war plan in general.

You have to know when to push back, and sometimes it helps

to explain why you're not giving information. In a briefing just days after the start of the Iraq war, there was intense interest in the rapid movement of U.S. forces toward Baghdad. General McChrystal was briefing with me that day. He talked about our forces crossing the Euphrates but made clear he did not want to go into detail about the route.

> *Q: General, the Iraqis obviously already know. Could you give us the furthest point of advance by say at least the Third Infantry and the First Mech. Just kind of pinpoint it a little bit for us on the map?*

There was an unwritten rule among briefers that you could and should jump in if you saw an opportunity or a problem coming.

> *Clarke: Let me jump in there for a second. Operations are on the way. A lot of parts and pieces are moving as we speak, and clearly strategic surprise—isn't something we've got. There is still tactical surprise, and we're going to try hard not to stand up here and paint a picture for the Iraqi regime of exactly where we are and exactly what we've got going at any moment of time.*

The reporters in the briefing room understood the rationale, but it never stopped them from trying to get us to say where we were going, how we were getting there, and when we'd arrive. Again, no hard feelings. That's their job. Not revealing information that could endanger our troops was mine. I always kept Joyce Rumsfeld's maxim in the back of my head, so I never minded their trying. It drove the viewing public batty. After most televised briefings, we were flooded by calls, e-mails, and faxes from the general public, many of them expressing the same thought: "How can those reporters be so stupid as to ask those questions?"

The reporters' frustration and the public's annoyance go right to the heart of the fundamental issue driving the media's relationship with those they cover. When does the public's right to know something outweigh somebody's privacy? When does the need to inform and educate the American people outweigh the need for operational security? There are no hard-and-fast rules. What's important is that each side respects the other's needs. Otherwise, "operational security" can become an excuse not to reveal information that people really do have a right to know, and the "right to know" can be used as a cloak for invading people's privacy or putting them at risk.

When I was first nominated for the job at the Pentagon, I began reading everything I could to try to get up to speed. Well, at least to get myself to a place where I didn't feel completely overwhelmed. Reading through testimonies of my predecessors and poring over articles about major conflicts in previous years, I was struck by how many problems had erupted between the military and the media over the years. There were commissions, investigations, panels, and boards of inquiry, all sporting similar titles: "The Military and the Media—What Went Wrong in (fill in here *Vietnam* or *Grenada* or *Panama* or *the Persian Gulf War*)." It seemed that every time there was a conflict the media wanted to cover, there was a fight over access and a subsequent investigation that consumed enormous amounts of my predecessors' time.

Prior to 9/11, I didn't think about that much. With the start of combat in Afghanistan in early October of 2001, how much and what kind of access to provide reporters became a front burner issue and a contentious one. Despite our best efforts—and because there were very few "boots on the ground" in the early weeks of the war—many in the media were unhappy with the access they got. Driving home at night, going over a day's events in my mind, sometimes I wondered when I would get sucked into the first "What Went Wrong" military-media commission of the twenty-first century. Determined to nip that possibility in the bud, I started reaching out to correspondents, bureau chiefs, and media analysts, seeking a constructive conversation on the access topic before it became a crisis.

In all those conversations, I was struck by how often people on both sides said things like, "How are we going to fix this?" or "How are we going to make both sides happy?" To me, those questions missed the point completely. The preamble to the Constitution calls for a common defense. The First Amendment guarantees freedom of the press. Both important, those goals can tug in opposite directions sometimes, and they should. It's a healthy tension that you want in a free society. Our challenge, I thought, was more appropriately to constantly fine-tune the balance between the competing needs than to erase the conflict completely. "If we're completely happy with all the coverage," I said in meetings and interviews, "and the media are completely happy with the access we give them, then I think we probably live in the old Soviet Union."

The tension will exist, I hope, and be a real—sometimes difficult—reminder of one of our country's greatest strengths, a free and largely unfettered press. I know many don't share my view. Again, maybe it goes back to my *Washington Star* experience or to my good fortune in working with some extraordinary journalists over the last twenty-five years. But I believe in what they do and want them to do their jobs to the best of their abilities. There are snakes among the media, just as there are in every walk of life, and there are also many, many individuals trying to do their jobs well in challenging times.

A point I shouldn't have to make but I will is this: above all, when you're dealing with the media, don't lie. It's wrong for the obvious reasons. It's also dumb. You'll probably get caught, and unlike in Major League Baseball, you won't get your wrist slapped for the first few offenses. The first lie you tell ruins your credibility forever. Reporters will forgive mistakes. They cannot—and should not—forgive deliberate attempts to mislead.

Even though the media will always be important, you can't count on them alone, nor should you. Fewer and fewer people get their news and information from "traditional" news sources, and the credibility of those sources is falling. The Project for Excellence in Journalism released a report in March of 2004 that, depending on your place in the communications universe, painted a gloomy or bright picture for information trends. The report found daily newspaper circulation down 11 percent since 1990, and evening news viewership down 28 percent since 1995. Only ethnic media alternatives and online media saw any growth. That's a challenge for mainstream news media but an opportunity for people seeking real precision in how they reach audiences.

The Bush-Cheney campaign's ground game—especially in Ohio—rightfully got much of the attention in the 2004 presidential election. Less noticed but equally effective was the media game, a multifaceted effort fully integrated with the overall strategy. Veteran political correspondent Dan Balz of the *Washington Post* was one of the few to notice. He wrote about it on November 19, 2004.

The Bush campaign developed what [campaign manager Ken] Mehlman described as "a very aggressive and very . . . different multimedia" strategy to disseminate its message, concluding that traditional media and major networks no longer have a monopoly on reaching voters.

The Bush campaign spent heavily on such nontraditional sources as national cable networks, African-American and Christian radio, and Spanish language media. The campaign bought local radio advertising adjacent to rush-hour traffic reports and beamed ads into health clubs with their own TV networks.

"A lot of young families get information not at the 7 o'clock news but at their 7 o'clock workout before they go home," he said.

I am confident the Bush-Cheney campaign's ability to target people with a high degree of precision had a real impact on the outcome.

It's hard enough for traditional news outlets to compete with an explosion of alternative sources. They also have to deal with the fact that fewer and fewer of their "customers" trust them. A 2004 Gallup poll said Americans' trust in the media had fallen to 43 percent, the lowest in decades. Everyone's got a theory as to why the media are less trustworthy. My Republican friends think people are tired of the left-wing bias, and my Democratic friends are convinced that readers and viewers are really fed up with all the corporate fascists who control the flow of news. In my experience, media institutions, like the government, are usually too disorganized to have a coherent conspiratorial bias. Still, the perception is out there.

Major media scandals—like the Jayson Blair affair at the *New York Times* and CBS's questionable documents regarding George W. Bush's National Guard service—haven't helped. Incidentally, you'd think the media, who are in the business of catching people screwing up, would know how to handle it when they do. Most of them don't. David Broder—a terrific journalist who runs an annual "Hits and Misses" column highlighting his mistakes from the previous year—is an exception, and a very trusted one to boot. But he's a rare voice of accountability in the media. My Republican friends may strike me down for saying it, but I think Dan Rather's a fine journalist. Still, he botched the National Guard story, and his defensiveness long after it became clear that he was wrong made things worse. Similarly, newspaper readers can't help but notice that when mistakes are splashed across page one, the corrections still appear buried on the inside of the paper.

I don't take pleasure in the demise of the fourth estate's credibility. I think an active press corps that tries hard to inform, educate, and expose is one of the best ways to maintain an honest government and healthy democratic society. Practically, though, you have to accept reality, and reality is that there are more ways to reach target audiences.

Your communications plans will be more complex but—if executed correctly—more effective as well. A good plan includes everything from direct contact to a strong Web presence to working with the news media and a few other odds and ends, depending on what you're trying to accomplish. And every element of the plan needs to be fully integrated with any paid media you might employ.

The best tool to have in your arsenal—at least the one you

should employ first—is a healthy dose of reality. How often have you heard people—especially politicians, it seems—say, "We just need to communicate our plan better. We've got the right programs, but we don't have the right message." Very often you hear these sorts of comments from political party leaders after they've gotten their fannies whipped in the polls or their budget proposals have tanked.

Maybe not, is what I think. Maybe the problem is that your program stinks, not how you've packaged it. That's why the best weapon is often a commitment to actually *do* something differently.

That became apparent at the National Cable Television Association (NCTA) in 1994 as member companies, eager to get past the policy horrors of the late 1980s and early '90s, worked with the trade association's head, Decker Anstrom, and the senior staff to identify their goals for their trade association. When I went to work for NCTA in 1993, I knew little about the industry. "We want to be seen as the telecommunications provider of the future," they said, most of them with straight faces. "Right now, we're delivering cable TV. Soon, it will be digital cable, high-speed Internet, and phone service." I knew enough to assess their goals as very ambitious back then.

Plagued by poor customer service for years, most cable operators had begun to address the problem, but the perception was still awful. Long the butt of jokes for late-night comedians and even the subject of a twisted movie, *The Cable Guy*, starring Jim Carrey, cable companies found it hard to shake the long-standing image. Some board members recognized reality more than others. But they all made clear their intent.

"Wow," I thought as I left one of my first meetings with the

NCTA's Executive Committee, "this is going to be a short career with the cable industry."

Desperate times can produce great things, and the board of the NCTA was smart enough to hire Decker Anstrom as the group's head in the summer of 1993. A graduate of Macalester College in Saint Paul, Minnesota, Decker worked in the Carter administration, first in the Office of Management and Budget, and then the personnel shop, a job that honed his people instincts and abilities to manage large egos. He fell in with those who became known—appreciatively—as the Mondale mafia, people like Jim Johnson and Mike Berman and other Washington powerhouses.

Now the head of Landmark Communications, headquartered in Norfolk, Virginia, Decker was a unique animal in Washington. He understood politics and he understood what it takes to run a business. You can find lots of the former and a few of the latter in D.C. but seldom find both traits in one person.

Decker and I differed politically but shared similar philosophies on communications, and we were glued at the hip on one thing in particular: research. Lots of it, and the more brutal the results, the better. Among Decker's smartest decisions was to have Peter Hart—in my opinion, the best pollster in the country—do all the research for the association. Peter has a unique ability to deliver bad news directly but in a compassionate way. And in the early 1990s, he did not have much good news for the cable companies on the image front. Back then, their desire to be the leading providers of advanced telecommunications services—a reality for several of them today—seemed like a dream. And a nightmare for the trade association staff.

When in doubt in Washington, form a committee. That's

exactly what we did. Decker convinced industry leaders like Joe Collins of Time Warner Cable and Ralph Roberts of Comcast (for whom I now work) to sign up for a newly formed NCTA Public Affairs Committee. Knowing we had some of the most creative business people in the industry, he also enlisted Michael Fuchs of HBO and now-deceased Tony Cox of Showtime to help out. I know none of them wanted to be on any committees, much less one with the herculean task of improving the cable industry's image, but they participated. They gave their time, their experience, and their company's resources to the job.

Given the internal and external challenges, we knew we needed even more help. So we reached out to three young guys in New York at the firm Shepardson, Stern and Kaminsky (SS&K). They call themselves a creatively driven strategic communications firm. Now I think "strategic communications" is one of the most overused and misunderstood phrases, but Lenny Stern and his partners get it. They know that communications has to be multifaceted and integrated with an organization's business plan. They know that words alone don't sell. They too are research addicts.

When I first encountered SS&K, their claim to fame was some good work for the cable industry and a few other odds and ends. Today, their talents and results-based plans have them serving as top communications strategists for the likes of Microsoft, UNICEF, Blue Cross/Blue Shield, and Nike, to name just a few.

Their smarts back then were obvious. Their willingness to take chances was admirable. Lenny would head the account for us, and I thought more than once that his intellect and humor would be a big help as we slogged through trying times with our member companies. More important to me than anything else, frankly, was that they had worked successfully for Lynn Yaeger of Time Warner Cable. One of the brightest minds in communications bar none, Lynn is tough as nails and demanded superior work (from her trade association as well as her consultants). If Lenny could make her happy, that was good enough for me. And if we hired Lynn's firm, we stood a much better chance of selling any campaign to our member companies. Sold. We hired SS&K, and it was one of our wiser decisions.

The problem we faced was obvious. Cable wanted to be the provider of high-tech services, but most people viewed it as a low-tech, unreliable monopolist. Even though some companies had made significant progress in improving customer service, the perception was a sizable roadblock. We needed something much bigger than words to break through. We couldn't just "talk the talk," we told ourselves and our member companies again and again. We had to "walk the walk" when it came to customer service.

And thus was born the "On Time Guaranteed" program. We'd overcome resistance with customer service guarantees and *then* tell cable's technology story. The guarantees were simple: if a service tech was late for an installation, it was free; if he showed up tardy for a service call, it was twenty dollars off the fee.

Getting to that "simple" program was no easy feat. The first time we briefed board members on the concept of a nationwide guarantee program, one of them looked at me and said, "You haven't been in this industry long enough to be thinking about another career, but maybe you should!" Sort of like with childbirth, you forget about the pain. But it was painful back then, convincing board members and cable system managers and CFOs and public relations staff to guarantee their work. The board had asked us for an image campaign; we responded with a significant change in their business operations.

Of great help was the fact that Lenny and the gang had a track record in exactly this area. Time Warner Cable's New York system had launched the "We Just Might Surprise You" campaign in an effort to break through customer cynicism. Tardy service calls got the customer a free month of cable. Knowing that form often follows function, SS&K developed a sharp ad campaign—"It Takes a Hell of a Lot to Surprise New Yorkers"—using New York Public Library lions brought to life and scuba-clad pizza delivery men to break through New York's information clutter.

It worked. And, as they say, if you can make it there, you can make it anywhere. That became our mantra with skeptical cable companies. As part of a major, national effort to get industry buy-in for the On Time Guaranteed program, we took Time Warner staff, including the New York City group president, Dick Aurelio, on the road to give their testimonials. There was no reason for hardened cable system managers to believe some Washington hacks trying to tell them how to run their businesses. But it was hard for them to dispute a guy like Aurelio, one of the most successful cable execs.

The hard work paid off, and the industry launched the On Time Guaranteed program in early 1995. Not that we questioned their companies' commitment, but we did have the major executives all participate in a news conference at one of the biggest trade shows to pledge—publicly—their company's participation.

Success flowed from several different sources. We treated internal communications as a critical element, perhaps the most critical. In addition to national and regional briefings for companies and their employees, we did video conferences, distributed newsletters with testimonials and case studies, provided marketing materials, and did troubleshooting for individual systems whenever we could.

We kept the trade and consumer media well-informed through interviews and briefings and supplied them with many of the same materials we sent the companies. Making sure people understood that the effort was much more than a campaign—that it was a change in the way we did business—was critical. By being as transparent as possible with the news media, by letting them see just how hard these very real and substantive changes were to execute, we began to get that message through.

The advertising was edgy—especially for an industry uncomfortable with marketing—and depended heavily on local cable systems' using their on-air availabilities for ads.

As ever, we heavily researched the actual "on time" record for service calls, as well as any impacts on cable's image. The results surprised all of us. It wasn't news that relatively few service calls were late. Cable companies had improved on this front—they still need to do more, I know—but it takes a long time for bad images to improve. What was surprising was a 30 percent awareness of the On Time Guaranteed program within one year of its launch. Cable's customer service rating went up 8 percent, and there was a 9 percent increase in the industry's image as a technology leader. As the Yankee Group put it, "For the first time in 8 years, the public is giving cable significantly higher marks for its service quality. . . . The [campaign] represents a turning point in improving cable's image."

Not everyone was thrilled. Not every system manager wanted

to embrace the guarantees even if his CEO had made a public pledge. What a shock: people in the field, ignoring "corporate." The day of the OTG launch, we held our breath and waited, wondering if all the planning and work would pay off. I got dozens of phone calls that day, mostly from people checking in to report good news or reporters prodding for any screwups. As I returned to my desk in the early afternoon after Decker had done several interviews, one message immediately caught my eye. It was from a general manager in the Midwest: "Guarantee program [expletive deleted]. Call within two hours or you owe $20!!"

One of the many internal battles was deciding what "window" would be used to determine whether or not a technician was late. Some companies had windows as narrow as an hour—say the tech will be there between nine and ten a.m., for instance. Some of them, no kidding, had "all day" windows. After much debate, we had settled on two hours as the appropriate window for the industry program. Not everybody supported that decision.

I called the manager, but he was out. I left a message but never heard back from him. Somewhat obsessed with returning phone calls—and riding high on the success of the program—that night I sat down and sent him a note. I apologized for missing his call, made understanding comments about how difficult it might be to execute the program, and enclosed a twenty-dollar bill as a recognition of my tardiness and—I thought—a sign of my sense of humor.

It's amazing how fast mail can travel sometimes. A few days later I got an envelope back from him. It had more expletives deleted on the note inside and the twenty-dollar bill, cut into pieces and covered in some sticky substance. Oh well.

If reality is the basis of your communications plan—and it

should be—another simple tool is one that should be used a lot but isn't: real-life contact with your key constituencies.

I'm a big believer in face-to-face communications: literally meeting with key constituencies on a periodic basis. Update them, keep them informed of your agenda, and address their concerns before they become crises. There's an old adage that you shouldn't talk to people just when you need something from them. Establishing a solid relationship can be advantageous when you *do* have the inevitable crisis. And even more valuable than talking to people can be going to them.

When I first went to work for the cable TV industry, I fully realized and openly acknowledged that I knew little about the business. Being willing to say "I don't know" can be a powerful communications tool that opens lots of doors. For the first few months at NCTA, I hit the road, meeting with people at all levels. The usual suspects were obvious; everyone knew to visit with the powers-that-be at Time Warner, TCI (then the largest operator), and Turner. Less obvious were the midsize and small operators, or what the networks then thought of as niche programmers.

One of the names on my list was Prime Cable in Austin, Texas, headed by Jerry Lindauer, a smart exec and former Marine. "I have been an NCTA member for years," Lindauer said to me when I walked into his office, "and this is the first time anyone from NCTA has ever come to see me!" He appreciated it and gave me lots of good advice in return, and I could always count on him for help and counsel for years to come.

The busier you get, the harder it is to find time to meet with people outside your immediate organization. The benefits are so great, you have to try. In addition to generating goodwill for actually caring about what people have to say (and you do have to be sincere!), regularly interacting with "outsiders" is one of the few ways to keep any perspective.

Think of the largest organization in which you've ever worked, and then reflect on the Pentagon for comparison. With about 2 million people as "employees" worldwide and a $400 billion plus annual budget, it dwarfs everything else, and the challenge of keeping your perspective is enormous. There is so much "incoming" on a daily basis—issues, meetings, e-mails, faxes, memos, calls—that it's hard for most people to look past the edge of their desks, much less have a grip on what's going on in the rest of the world.

That's one very good reason why we fought to carve out time at the Pentagon for Rumsfeld and other senior officials— me included—to meet regularly with people from outside the building and beyond the military. After 9/11, the crush of a "normal" day turned into a daily tsunami, and it became even harder to maintain perspective. One thing I did do, without fail, was to call three or four friends every week on my way home at night. They all lived in different parts of the country and worked in nonmilitary professions.

"What's happening out there?" I'd regularly ask them. "What are people focused on? What are we missing?"

Most of the time their answers were pretty obvious. "The Yankees are winning" seemed to break through depressingly often. Many times, though, their distance from my daily life gave them important perspective on our issues and our communications efforts.

The near-obsession many people had with capturing bin Laden after 9/11 came through loud and clear—including from a pacifist friend who offered to "pull the switch myself if we get the SOB." The sentiment was understandable, but the single-minded focus on bin Laden was a problem. The threat from terrorists—to this day—is not about one man or one group. al Qaeda alone has cells in fifty or sixty different countries, and it was important for people to know that the war on terror would not end with one man's capture or death.

Instinctively, I knew that. Rumsfeld knew it for sure. But my connection with real people helped me make the case that we had to balance Americans' justifiable rage at bin Laden with the realities of the long war ahead.

The higher one makes it in the corporate or public world, the more tenuous the grip on reality. That's a problem. I think every CEO should try to interact with real people as often as possible. Attend focus groups of actual customers at least once a year, preferably more, and hear what real people have to say about your product. Don't just read the analyses of highly paid consultants who may or may not want to deliver the honest assessment if it's a harsh one.

The importance of human contact will never change, unlike information technologies, which evolve constantly. And the change is so fast, it's impossible to say which tool will work and when five or ten years from now. But the best principles will remain the same. As people have more information choices— and as they get more comfortable using those new devices—you have to employ what works for each audience. And don't bother with what doesn't work.

A few years ago, a record company executive shared his concerns with me about the explosion in the illegal downloading of music. He and others were contemplating the pros and cons of legal action against piraters and the creators of the new technologies that make it easy for millions of users to steal music. This exec was focused on a public service campaign directed at teenagers and intended to spell out the consequences of illegal downloading.

"Take Pittsburgh, for example," he said to me, not knowing I was from there. "We need a really hard-hitting op-ed in the *Pittsburgh Post-Gazette* that drives home that this is stealing—plain and simple."

I appreciated his zeal but was surprised that a guy who successfully sold lots of music to kids—all the stealing notwithstanding—had so little sense of how you'd reach them. "I don't spend much time in Pittsburgh these days," I said, "but unless things have changed a lot, I don't think too many seventeen-year-olds read the editorial pages of the *Post-Gazette*." Showing up at the local skateboard park with free Red Bull and some local musicians to drive home the message might work better, I offered.

If young people are hard to influence, it's close to impossible to reach people in Washington. They're a high-value target and subject to a lot of incoming. Public officials and their staff are exposed to a vast array of messages from interest groups, media, and cranky constituents. Unsurprisingly, they're hardened and immune to most messages.

That's what we faced in the mid-'90s as the cable TV industry embarked on another ambitious effort. We had to convince policy makers, especially a select group of congressmen and their staffs, that we were committed to better service, that our technology was increasingly cutting-edge, and that we had a sincere desire to see America's schools and libraries enter the Information Age.

The industry underwent real changes after the reregulation of the early '90s. Midsize companies—incapable of withstanding the new rules and regulations—had mostly sold out. Big companies got bigger and small ones wondered if it was just a matter of time before they got eaten up. Cable networks, once a small handful led by stars like HBO and Discovery, began to flourish and set the standards for creative and often edgy programming.

Thanks to the On Time Guaranteed program and individual company efforts, many of the major companies felt more confident that they were handling customer service problems and perceptions better than before.

Things felt good, but the NCTA gang was never one to rest on its laurels. Nor would our member companies ever let us. Knowing they wanted to move into additional lines of telecom business—high-speed Internet and phone service for example—the cable execs and Decker Anstrom knew that we'd need the most favorable policy environment possible.

After some discussion and debate, the NCTA board agreed to a campaign designed specifically to create a more favorable environment in which policy makers viewed cable. It would not tackle individual issues or pieces of legislation, but if it made it easier for Congress to provide some deregulation of the industry, that would be just fine.

For this, we enlisted Carter Eskew and Jamie Sterling. Their firm at the time was Bozell-Eskew, a corporate image and issues advocacy firm (where I went to work after NCTA). Carter, the creative guy, and Jamie, the media buyer, both cut their teeth on political campaigns and had segued into the challenging world of issues advocacy work for corporations. They had impressive results working for Microsoft (starting to feel the heat from Washington in the mid-'90s) and the pharmaceutical industry (keen to ensure that people knew how much they invested in research and development). The only doubt in my mind was whether Bozell-Eskew could really work outside the box, take the typical constraints of working for a trade association and produce a campaign with real impact.

As a matter of fact, I had my own doubts that *anybody* could break through in a meaningful way with Washington policy makers. Proud of the earlier cable industry campaign—with its substantive centerpiece—I was worried about promising more than we could deliver to our member companies.

Our campaign messages—admittedly more believable to some than others—were easy to craft. On the communications front, what would be harder than crafting the message would be finding ways to break through to audiences not inclined to hear *anything*. That's where Peter Hart's help was invaluable. He conducted a series of focus groups with Capitol Hill staffers to determine what kind of communications vehicles worked. What broke through and why? What messages were more effective than others and why?

Peter always strives to get genuine responses and reactions from people, rather than leading them to a hoped-for conclusion. "Tell me what advocacy or issue campaigns resonated the most with you over the last year or so," Peter asked the first group in an open-ended fashion. "Who really had an impact on you?"

Focus group participants almost always start out quietly and pick up steam as they go along. Seldom were Peter's first questions met with total silence, though. At first those of us on the other side of the mirror thought maybe they hadn't heard Peter. Maybe they were really tired. Then, as Peter pushed, it became clear: despite lives that centered around policy, politics, and advocacy, these well-connected Hill staffers couldn't recall much, if anything, about massive campaigns that were designed to reach people exactly like them. *Nobody* had reached them. They couldn't remember the tobacco industry's ads or the pharmaceutical companies' or the paper industry's, despite the fact that those industries and others were spending hundreds of millions of dollars every year in an effort to influence them.

Peter never gives up. "Come on, you must be able to recall something," he good-naturedly prodded.

Finally, one staffer raised his head with a happy look on his face. "Hey, remember that really cool Nerf football that somebody sent around the Hill with their logo and ad on it?" Several other faces lit up around the table.

"Oh yeah," another one said. "That was great. We threw that thing around forever."

The once sleepy and grumpy focus group turned into a raucous recollection of who got the best trinket from which organization. Hats were a big hit if they were good quality, but "not those cheesy ones with the plastic tabs in the back," they all agreed. Anything you could feel and hold and throw was a winner. Being able to eat something was good too.

As that focus group broke up and staff cleaned up for the next round, Peter came into the room where we sat for his frequent fix of M&M's.

"The answer," he said, with a big smile on his face, "is tchotchkes."

Tchotchkes. Trinkets. Toys.

Several other focus groups with Washington "influencers" confirmed what we heard in the first group. These people— influential staffers to important federal officials—were so numb to the thousands of "traditional" means to reach them, they only truly responded to the unconventional. So we embraced unconventional to the hilt. Our advocacy would look different and show up in startling color and unusual places. The game plan was simple yet different from anything ever done before in Washington: turn traditional advocacy on its head to break through. Guided by some very smart people at Bozell-Eskew, that's exactly what we did.

Start with the color. In a depressingly familiar attempt to appear "in," most advocacy efforts targeted at policy makers look like something produced for the Congressional Record—black, white, and maybe some gray thrown in for good measure. Heavy emphasis on text. Few or no visuals. In short, pretty ugly stuff.

Not us. Our core message ("Cable TV—Wired to the Future") and its elements showed up in eye-opening shades of hot pink, lime green, orange, and electric blue.

Our communications vehicles were different too. Most Washington campaigns center on ads in some pretty typical (and expensive) places—the Federal Page of the *Washington Post,* for example, inside *Congressional Quarterly,* or on the back of *Roll Call,* the Capitol Hill paper seen on every staffer's desk. We did some of that—the bare minimum. But we wanted to show up in an environment in which our target audiences' defenses against advocacy messages might not be on "high."

So we showed up on the sides of buses. Usually the platform for movies or shows coming to Washington, several area Metrobuses sported our ads in their shocking colors. We appeared in key subway stops—Eastern Market, Capitol South, and Union Station, all stops used heavily by Hill staffers.

And we gave them tchotchkes. Like they'd never seen before. We gravitated toward what we heard in the focus groups: people remembered what they could feel and play with at their desks. Our first tchotchke was a small beanbag toy named Viewy. Sporting arms, legs, and the logo, Viewy went to several thousand carefully targeted policy makers on the Hill and in agencies, their key staffers, and—just to keep them in the loop—select media that covered the industry. A big hit, Viewy was followed up by a stress squeeze toy and a small Wired to the Future basketball hoop and ball that could go on the backs of doors and rims of trash cans. To this day, I can walk into offices in Washington and still see Viewys and hoops.

One of the cleverest—and most impact-packed—tchotchkes was the cube. It looked a lot like a Rubik's cube; on each side were graphic images that demonstrated our core messages and blared the vibrant colors that became a hallmark of the campaign. Turn the cube in any direction and you found another message about the industry's commitment to service or education or technological advances. People could not put it down.

Internet advertising was in its infant stages back then, but we did show up on some relevant sites with quick messages. We doubted the ads would actually influence anybody's thinking directly, but our willingness to show up where others didn't added to the "boy, this is something different" atmosphere.

Creativity dictated the content of the campaign. Thriftiness and surgical precision determined where it appeared. Trade association members are notorious for not wanting to spend much marketing dollars on industrywide campaigns, and NCTA's

members were no different. They gave us a pool of money to spend above and beyond anything they had committed before, but it wasn't at the level of, say, the tobacco industry. We were going to have to make it stretch.

That's where Jamie Sterling became the secret weapon. Good-looking and supplied with endless time and energy for friends, Jamie is the best media buyer in the business. I think you could call any TV station, network, or newspaper in the country, and the ad sales people there will know him. More importantly, they will all say how much they like dealing with Jamie. He's honest, he's direct, and he knows his business.

As Jamie himself would tell you, there are a lot of smart media buyers. Plenty of them have lots of experience. What sets him apart from the rest of the pack is his honesty. He will tell you the truth, not rip you off, and work hard for you every single day.

Early on, I realized how important Jamie was to the cable effort. To get the most out of our innovative campaign, the buys had to be as creative as the content. Every dollar had to have maximum impact.

Jamie delivered. He didn't just get our ads onto bus sides— a first—but he researched which routes were viewed most often by staffers traveling to and from Capitol Hill. He got us on *Imus in the Morning,* which was hugely popular with everyone in Washington—even if they tell you otherwise—but he didn't waste our money on the typical drive time of seven to nine a.m. The kinds of people we hoped to reach were at work already by eight; we didn't need or want many of those people toddling in at nine.

Everyone is familiar with the wall ads in airport terminals. Until Cable TV—Wired to the Future, few in Washington had

ever seen industry advocacy ads appear in the hallways and at the baggage claims of (then) Washington National Airport.

And no one in Washington had seen the kinds of TV ads that we did. To break through the clutter and the numbness, we had to do TV that was dramatically different. No talking heads for this campaign, or so-called credible third parties standing in front of the U.S. Capitol.

Carter Eskew and his creative team produced stop-you-in-your-tracks spots. One called "Kids Heads" asked the question, "How does cable TV make education come alive for our children?" and answered it with gorgeous, swirling images of historical figures, famous antiquities, current events, authors, art masterpieces, animals, and more coming out of the kids' heads. Rather than boring words and static images—pretty standard stuff for Washington campaigns—these ads found the most compelling ways to demonstrate cable's commitment to education and, by the way, the fact that kids could download things from the Internet fifty to one hundred times faster on cable than by a phone line.

Returning from an event on the West Coast, I swung past baggage claim at National on my way to grab a cab home. Familiar music caught my attention, and I looked up at the monitor over the baggage carousel. Jamie did a buy on those airport monitors because of the CNN effect. People—including members of Congress—tended to glance at the screens as they headed to and from planes, hoping to catch a bit of news.

As I looked up, I saw a group of well-dressed folks staring at the screen with smiles on their faces. It was our "Boy Who Loves Whales" spot, in which young students making papier-mâché whales morph into one boy finding incredible scenes and infor-

mation about real whales online. Of course, he can get better images and get them faster, thanks to cable's high-speed Internet capabilities, the spot helpfully pointed out.

"I had no idea cable could do that," said one traveler as he picked up his bag. "That's pretty cool."

That's pretty amazing, I thought as I headed home. Who knows who that guy is, but the campaign worked on him!

It did work. People—especially those we targeted—saw the campaign and liked it. More important, despite a relatively small buy, the campaign   coupled with hard government and public affairs activities—made a difference. Slowly but surely, the Washington opinion of cable started to improve. As measured by the brutally honest Peter Hart, the innovative advocacy campaign contributed to that shift.

It wasn't ads alone that changed the mood about cable and awareness of cable's accomplishments. It was those tactics, working hand in glove with other communications tools, including direct, face-to-face contact, work with the trade and consumer media, and simple Internet outreach, that made the difference.

When we did Cable TV: Wired to the Future, using the Internet was new, and expectations about its efficacy were low. In the early '90s, few organizations had their own Web sites, and mainstream news media saw the Internet as not much more than a high-tech meeting place for geeks. Barely a decade later, Web sites are the norm and news managers struggle daily to maintain a robust online presence in a 24/7 instantaneous news environment and to react to "news" broken by bloggers.

Increasingly, consumer behavior is shifting to a "what I want, when and how I want it" mentality. It's true in information too, and the Internet is a big part of that shift. Before, just having a

Web site relatively easy to navigate was considered good. Now, your site needs to address that "me" mentality and give users current and engaging content, e-mail lists and alerts, subscriber functions, and highly customizable search capabilities.

Before you throw all your communications eggs in one online basket, know that the story isn't the same everywhere. The Pew Internet & American Life Project gave insights on the demographics of Internet use. Internet usage is highest in the Pacific Northwest and lowest in the South. California has the highest percentage of minorities online, but the Washington, D.C., area has the highest African-American usage. So if you're trying to reach a southern audience, that information would tell you to soft-pedal the Internet presence and beef up in other areas. If you were trying to reach African Americans in the nation's capital, you'd know the Internet would be an important part of the strategy.

Research and data instruments available today allow you to fine-tune those broad regional assessments into clear pictures of who's doing what informationwise on a neighborhood-by-neighborhood basis. Sound like a lot of work? Maybe. But by seeking that kind of precision, you far more efficiently allocate your resources and increase the likelihood of achieving your goals.

Adapt one of the more successful lines from the 1992 Clinton campaign and you get to the essence of the Internet's power: "It's about me, stupid." Increasingly pressed for time and resources, people want to know what's most relevant to them and their families. The Internet makes that easier than ever. People can get more information straight from the source—rather than through a filter—and the technology allows an organization to provide a volume and complexity of information not readily communicated in written or oral presentations.

Despite the Internet's technological edge, the fundamentals of communication remain the same. For example, one of my favorites: keep everything as simple as possible, but not one bit simpler. Avoid jargon whenever possible. Be current.

Despite some good intentions, the Pentagon's online presence pretty much violated every one of those rules prior to 2001. It really was the Pentagon—through the Defense Advanced Research Projects Agency—that created the Internet. The creators and their successors were geniuses, but I swear English must have been a second language for some of them. They spoke in terms no mere mortal could understand. There were literally thousands of DOD Web sites—so many that nobody knew the real number—and most of them were masses of complex information communicated in long, unwieldy sentences and crowded with busy charts and diagrams.

DefenseLINK.mil was the "face" of the Pentagon, the main Web site on which—supposedly—one could get basic information about the Pentagon, the services, defense contracts, and related issues. Thanks to the hard work of people like Navy Captain Tim Taylor, the Web site had been getting better since it first launched in 1994. Bureaucracy is a powerful force, though, one incredibly resistant to change, and progress was minimal. Making that Web site more user-friendly was one of many things I put on my long list of long-term objectives for my time at the Pentagon.

Until 9/11, that goal was not a top priority. We were trying to figure out how to get people to care about the military, period, and we had more fundamental issues to address. In many ways, 9/11 changed everything. Within hours of the attacks, we were inundated with thousands and thousands of requests for information from the general public. They called, wrote, e-mailed, and faxed at all hours of the day and night. For the first several weeks, their interest was in the Pentagon and the people who had been killed or hurt there. After the start of military operations, October 7, 2001, their questions turned to the forces and their operations. How many people do we have there? What kind of ships and firepower are they using? How will our forces handle the coming winter and bad weather?

Their interests were not dramatically different from those of the news media, but clearly the American people had a thirst for information about the military that went beyond what the news media gave many of them. And we weren't helping them much. Savvier folks managed to figure out how to navigate DefenseLINK to find the briefing transcripts and some DOD photos produced by Combat Camera. But the average guy on the street needed something different.

In the midst of everything else, I started asking colleagues about how we could get a very different kind of Web site done, quickly. Despite the challenges of the time—we were at war, for God's sake, and there was a huge gash in one side of the Pentagon—some people didn't think an urgent need for information should get in the way of bureaucracy. The "why we can't do that quickly" replies were lengthy but consistent.

"Especially now, we have real security concerns about firewalls," the guys from Command, Control, Communications and Information (C3I) would say.

"The budget didn't take this need into account," said the comptroller's office. (No kidding, I thought.)

The list went on and on. Nothing got done. I was frustrated but too busy with everything else going on to focus too hard on the issue. And then every once in a while, you think to yourself, Better to beg forgiveness than ask permission. On a Sunday in mid-October of '01, not long after the start of combat operations, I came back to my office in the Pentagon from a round of meetings upstairs. As I surfed through a pile of messages, I saw one from Dave Jackson with a northern Virginia phone number on it. Dave was an old friend who had worked for *Time* magazine in several different placcs, including a stint as the Hong Kong bureau chief and the head of *Time*'s San Francisco office. From what I had seen and heard, my old friend, who was the furthest thing from a geek, had become quite the techno wiz, understanding more than the finances of the dot-com world. Evidently, he actually knew what made the stuff work. I hadn't talked with him for a while, but I assumed that *Time* had brought him in to reinforce their troops on the East Coast covering the aftermath of the 9/11 attacks and the subsequent military action.

I placed his call first, thinking it might be one of the more pleasant calls of the day.

"What are you up to?" I asked when I reached him at his in-laws' house.

Dave told me that he had recently taken a buyout from *Time* and had come east with his wife, Susan, and daughter to figure out their next move. Necessity being the mother of invention, an idea popped into my head.

"What are you doing right now?" I asked him.

"I just told you," Dave said, a little exasperated at my lack of attention. "We're back east trying to figure out what we'll do next."

"No, I mean *right* now," I said, "as in this afternoon."

I quickly told Dave my problem on the Web site front and asked him if he could give up his Sunday afternoon to come in and talk with me and a few others about it. Dave's good nature, coupled with his desire—shared by many—to contribute in some fashion had him in my office in a few minutes.

"Who are you trying to reach?" he asked us.

"Real people," we answered. "Not the military experts."

"What do you want the look and feel to be?"

"User-friendly. Workmanlike. Professional without being slick."

"What are you trying to convey?"

"The tremendous work being done by the men and women of the armed forces."

Dave then launched into a lengthy description of mistakes most people made in developing Web sites, what worked and what didn't, all based on his considerable experience.

"So tell me how we can get this done," I interrupted Dave, fully expecting him to tell me he'd get back to me in a few days with the names of a few people we might hire.

"Well, I could do it," came the surprising response. "I'd need insiders who have the real information to turn into content, and a technical person who can help me figure out how we'd piggyback on the Pentagon system, but I could do it."

It took me about ten seconds to make a decision. I called Pat Bursell, our budget and admin chief (and a true class act), and asked her to come in as soon as possible. Pat didn't ask why; she got there in under an hour despite the fact she hadn't had a weekend off in several weeks.

"Pat, I need you to get this guy paid somehow, I need you

to help him find his way through the IT mazes of this place, and it has to be done fast. And make sure everything is legal and aboveboard."

Pat handled the logistics, and Dave did what everyone else I approached on the challenge said couldn't be done. Working with a small but dogged team, he had a new Web site, Defend-America, up within days.

Given the intense public interest in all things Pentagon then, it didn't take much more than word of mouth (and e-mail) for people to find the site. The public responses were uniformly positive, and even those in the news media who cover the online world took notice. *USA Today* cited DefendAmerica as the "hot site" of the week early on, and some of Dave's former colleagues at *Time* took notice, writing, "If you want the official war news, that's easy—go to the Pentagon's comprehensive site, *www.DefendAmerica.mil.*"

DefendAmerica isn't for everybody. It doesn't have the depth of information that some heavy-duty Pentagon watchers seek. But it filled a need at a critical time, giving us yet another tool to use to reach some of the American people with whom we were not connecting. And it's had some side benefits as well. Thanks to the positive reaction to DefendAmerica, slowly but surely, a determined band of IT experts have managed to improve the look and navigation and content of the main DOD Web site, DefenseLINK.mil.

When Dave built DefendAmerica, most Internet users focused on the now relatively mundane surfing of Web sites and a few dedicated souls spent time in chat rooms. What a difference a few years makes. "Blog readership shoots up 58% in 2004," reads the headline of a report issued by the Pew Internet & American Life Project. "But 62% of online Americans do not know what a blog is."

That kind of sums up my feelings on blogs. I know more and more people have them, that 7 percent of the 120 million U.S. adults who use the Internet say they've created them, according to Pew, but I'm not yet sure what their real, long-term role will be.

Clearly they've *had* an impact. Whether with political "coverage," commentary on the Laci Peterson trial, or firsthand accounts from victims of the tsunami in Southeast Asia, blogs' impact prompted Merriam-Webster to name *blog* word of the year in 2004, and ABC News named bloggers their "People of the Year."

There are cautions to be sure before one embraces blogs as the "killer app" of new communications technologies. They're in the growing category of "straight from the horse's mouth" sentiment, but they have problems too. There are no filters, no real fact-checkers, no credentials for the bloggers and their stated expertise on any subject.

John Schwartz of the *New York Times* suggested in an article in early 2005 that there is often a "self-correcting" aspect to blogs. After recounting some of the wilder rumors and conspiracy theories regarding the cause of the catastrophic tsunami, Schwartz demonstrated that after the initial rounds of far-fetched ideas and their accompanying ridicule, "the follow-up comments were a sober discussion of what actually causes earthquakes."

There's no denying blogs' influence thus far. Bloggers first "broke" Trent Lott's comments at Senator Strom Thurmond's birthday party that resulted in Lott's ouster as Senate majority leader. The *60 Minutes* story on President Bush's National Guard service that CBS broadcast a month and a half before the 2004 election was challenged as it was airing by bloggers who actually had real-life experience with the kinds of typewriters that would have been in use during Bush's service.

The questions to ask as you develop a communications plan are obvious: What do we do about the bloggers? Do we treat them like regular journalists? Do we ignore them, even if they get information wrong? What about employees that use blogs to criticize their employers under a cloak of anonymity? Do we create our own as a way to reach people?

The tougher questions are really for the mainstream news media—or msm, as the bloggers shorthand it. How do they distinguish themselves from blogs as a source of credible information? Do they react—and sometimes overreact—to news "broken" on blogs?

There are societal questions too. Although the research on blogs is new and sketchy, it seems clear that people spend most time with other bloggers who share their views and interests. It's water seeking its own level, I guess, but those who regularly frequent blogs draw comfort from those who agree with them and offer encouragement. It's a little ironic that the very technology that gives people the ability to reach and experience limitless sources of information, views, and experiences may lead them, instead, to a very narrow band on the spectrum of ideas.

But enough about society. Back to you and what you do about it. First of all, as confusing and sometimes annoying as the blogs may be, pay attention. Many of them, depending on your field, do have an impact. Maybe it's directly with your customers; maybe it's with the trade and consumer media that cover your industry. And just as you address any new development that impacts your business, you need to deal with the influential bloggers in your world. Every situation will be different, but if you monitor them—and pay attention to your key constituencies—you'll quickly discover which deserve your organization's attention. As John Schwartz pointed out, the blogger community has a self-correcting aspect which will help you decide which ones are credible and which aren't.

There are no formal organizations or code of ethics among bloggers—although there's a school of thought and discussion suggesting that such an approach might be worthwhile. And I am not sure how the First Amendment applies to bloggers, but I am sure there will be a legal case on that one of these days soon. But I think you can informally apply the same standards to bloggers that you use in the "mainstream" world. Are you—or someone you trust—familiar with the person's work? Has a particular blog previously had an impact on a significant issue in your world? Based on those and other admittedly informal criteria, you can make an educated guess as to how much time you should devote to any particular blog.

There are lots of potential problems with blogs, I know. If a blogger gets something wrong and won't fix it, to whom do you complain? You often don't even know who a blogger is, so how can you or anybody else hold him or her accountable?

There are two hard-core realities about blogs. First, they're out there, and they're reaching more people every day. Second, there's only so much you can do to influence them. Those realities and the surrounding confusion put even more emphasis on the need for you to tell your own story, in as robust and comprehensive a fashion as possible. There's a huge vacuum of information out there, and if you're not doing your best to fill it, others—including bloggers—will.

Sometimes I look back twenty or thirty years in the communications business and think, Boy, things were a lot simpler then. The explosion of information technologies makes the business more complex, for sure, but the fundamentals are clear:

- Know your audiences and know what works for them. Don't get frustrated that the kid in Pittsburgh won't read your op-ed. Meet him on his ground—the skate-board park—and maybe you can convince him to show your op-ed to his parents.
- Use multiple tools to reach people. Breaking through the daily crush of information overload requires a comprehensive and sustained effort.
- And finally, get comfortable with the notion that you have to operate outside your comfort zone. Because the one constant in communications is change. Technology and competition will ensure that just as you've gotten comfortable in one arena—say you've really figured out how to handle blogs—a new one will arise.

CHAPTER 4

Time to Get a Bigger Monkey

---

*Unusual times require
unusual tactics.*

As U.S. trade representative from 1989 to 1993, Carla A. Hills left no stone unturned. Intense and with a well-deserved reputation for always being phenomenally well prepared, Carla was convinced the path to success in trade policy would be to convince a wide swath of people—above and beyond the business community—that aggressive policies that "opened markets to expand trade" (affectionately known in the USTR's office as OMET) would benefit all. She was right, and she was ahead of her time.

So few people understood or appreciated the often-complex

world of trade that early in her tenure, we had buttons printed up that said, "The Uruguay Round Is Not a Dance." No two ways about it, enlightening nontrade wonks about the benefits of trade would be an uphill challenge.

Getting that new round of multilateral trade negotiations would be an especially tough task, as would the perennial fight in Congress over "fast track," which assures our trading partners that Congress won't reopen agreements once they've been negotiated. The usual forces lined up on either side, business for it and labor, consumer groups, and human rights advocates often against it.

Carla knew how to push the edge of the envelope, and she knew that just reaching the conventional audiences—economists or financial writers—wouldn't do it. She challenged the public affairs and legislative staff to forge relationships with new constituencies, groups not normally associated with protrade positions or even trade at all, for that matter. Hispanics for Fast Track, she suggested. Veterans for Fast Track. It became an obsession for me: think of every group possible that might influence the people we wanted influenced—namely, Congress. I started looking through the phone book under "associations" for inspiration.

I didn't go to church much back then, but I did walk past many of them on Sundays when I would go into the office to try and catch up and get ahead. I never did. During my Pentagon time, people often asked me, "How can you work for a guy like Rumsfeld?" assuming, correctly, that he was a demanding sort. After working for Carla Hills, you can do anything.

The phone book turned up few prospects, but the churches did. Somehow, we discovered that the U.S. Conference of Catholic Bishops had been having internal discussions about trade in general and fast track in particular. Labor was pressuring them to take a stand, and the bishops—generally perceived as liberal on economic issues—were mulling it over.

One might ask why the bishops would care about trade. But then one could ask a lot of questions about the conference, including why they have an Office of Film and Broadcasting in New York. With 350 employees and nearly four dozen committees, including domestic, international, and trade policy, the conference got into a lot of things.

Thus was born my public affairs "Holy Grail."

"We're going to get Bishops for Fast Track," I announced to Carla and some of her senior staff. "They're smart, influential in their communities, and they're leaders to whom some members of Congress might listen." Carla and team listened, but I think most of them thought I was nuts.

We papered the conference with briefing materials. We gave them testimonial after testimonial from other groups on behalf of fast track. They didn't budge. After several weeks of advocacy, it was still unclear if they would take any position at all. If they did, it seemed likely they would go against us.

Then the conference came up with a wonderful idea. Given their keen interest in the topic and their stated desire to be as informed as possible, they asked Carla and Tom Donahue, then secretary-treasurer of the AFL-CIO, to debate before the Administrative Committee, over fifty bishops representing the leadership and thirteen regions.

A classic Irish pol, Donahue represented the best of labor. Smart and dedicated, he headed USTR's Labor Advisory Committee. Despite disagreeing with many of our policies, he always engaged with humor and decency, but fiercely. Tom joined the

Navy when he was seventeen, got his law degree while working for the Building Services Employees International Union in New York City, was labor coordinator for Radio Free Europe and the Free Europe Committee in Paris in the late 1950s. He had seen a lot. Best of all, he was a fabulous storyteller, and you wanted to be buying him a drink at the airport while you waited on yet another delayed flight to Brussels.

The debate was in Northeast Washington on a beautiful day. Predebate negotiations dictated that there would be no media present and few staff. Hills and Donahue would each address the bishops for ten minutes and then take questions for another forty.

With sunlight streaming through stained-glassed windows, Carla and Tom launched into amazing performances. Listening to them I thought, "What a shame more people can't hear this." When you know trade, it's not as dry as it sounds. These two had a high-level, thoughtful, engaging, and provocative debate, fueled by interesting and original questions from the bishops.

The bishops decided not to take a stand on the issue. I couldn't print up "Bishops for Fast Track" buttons, but I considered it a win nonetheless. The bishops may not have endorsed us, but they didn't take a stand against fast track either—as many might initially have expected them to do.

Going to the unusual suspects broadens your base of support. Sometimes they're the only ones who will listen.

In the cable world, Decker Anstrom "got" communications better than most. He had a keen appreciation for the industry's substantive accomplishments and for how and to whom we communicated them. Having seen formerly friendly policy makers go south on cable when things got tough, Decker set out to ensure that cable had a wide base of support from which it could operate. That meant going beyond the usual suspects, like relevant congressional committees and FCC commissioners and staff. Heck, some of those people wouldn't talk to us, so we *really* needed to reach out.

In the early '90s, as the industry tried to dig its way out from new regulation, it also embarked on developing new technologies, like using its "fat" broadband pipe to deliver high-speed Internet service and phone service. The challenge was multifaceted. Although the industry's reputation was improving, many people still thought of cable as an antiquated technology and weren't ready to embrace it as a provider of state-of-the-art services. Many policy makers thought we'd be better off sticking to our knitting—that is, fixing the service and keeping rates down.

Sometimes being lucky is better than being smart. At the very time that we were looking for people to listen to our story about the new cable industry, the education community was addressing what was called the "digital divide." Education leaders nationwide were understandably concerned that many children, especially in low-income and underserved areas, would miss out on the benefits of the information era.

Decker was the son of two high school teachers, so he understood where the educators and parents were coming from. He saw their need, and he recognized an opportunity. In 1996 the cable industry, under Decker's leadership, launched a huge initiative to wire every school and library in the country with free, high-speed Internet access. As cable companies rolled out Internet service in a community, they would go into each school and library at the same time. Given the varying pace with which cable companies would introduce the new service, not all schools and libraries would benefit right away. But they did benefit in time. As of 2005, 78 percent of the K–12 public and private schools had gotten high-speed online service.

In the first-ever positive editorial about the cable industry, the *New York Times* called the program "Cable's Gift to Schools" and said that the offer "will bring fabulous educational resources to schools too poor to provide an advanced Internet hookup on their own." Better than the *NYT* editorial was the new relationship with a new constituency. Thousands of teachers, librarians, and parents had new reason to think differently about the cable industry.

That initiative and others, like the media literacy program developed with the Parent Teachers Association (PTA), created a firm foundation for the cable industry. On controversies like TV violence or Janet Jackson's "wardrobe malfunction," the industry has a reservoir of support on which it can draw. That doesn't mean that every teacher loves the industry. It does mean that cable industry leaders and employees can get an audience with them.

Getting audiences was never hard at the Pentagon. Getting the right audiences was another matter. For years, the drill included the SecDef and other Pentagon leadership meeting with industry officials, retired officers, and veterans organizations—for the most part, groups you could count on.

Before 9/11, my biggest challenge was getting other people to care about the military. Fewer and fewer people had real-life experience with the military. Given the aging population (one thousand World War II veterans die every day) and the limited number of military conflicts, few people outside the "immediate family" had any interest in or knowledge of the armed forces. That might be okay if nothing bad happened, or if we anticipated few changes to the normal course of business. But that would not be the case under Secretary Rumsfeld. His intense focus on transforming the Pentagon so it could meet the very unconventional challenges of the twenty-first century meant a lot of china would be broken.

Most people don't like change. Few like it less than those entrenched in the *business* of defense. Defense contractors, veteran congressional staffers, and career civilian and military staffers would oppose the SecDef on everything from base closings and outdated weapons systems to overhauling the outdated personnel management system. Clearly this was a case in which the usual suspects not only wouldn't help us; they were part of the problem. Thus began the development of an aggressive and comprehensive outreach program.

We knew how to find the usual suspects—the retired flag officers who appear often on television, the think tank analysts. Harder to find would be those people who—especially prior to 9/11—got up every day not thinking much about the Pentagon or the men and women in uniform. Business and civic leaders wouldn't be too hard: many of us knew people with the U.S. Chamber of Commerce or manufacturing trade associations. But we knew that wouldn't be enough. If there was to be sustained support for major change throughout the Department of Defense worldwide, we would have to cast the net wider.

We started to find people in education, in trade. We sought out minority organizations, like the National Council of La Raza (NCLR), arguably the nation's largest and most effective Hispanic organization. As Hispanics increase in the general population, they also have begun to swell the ranks of the military, and we thought those who represented them should know what we were all about. And they should know the very changes we promoted would benefit their constituencies. Take BRAC, for example. If you shed the department's excess facilities and their accompanying costs, you can better spend that money on equipment and training. Our arguments for change were sound, but the interest beyond our immediate circles was small.

Some people got it—people like Raul Yzaguirre, then the head of NCLR. I first met him when I was at USTR. We had mud-wrestled with the White House political office to add Hispanics and environmentalists to our private sector advisory system, and Raul was one of our best adds. He was a good friend of the agency back then and a good friend to me, the secretary, and others as we tried to reach out to diverse constituencies.

Sadly, he was an exception. Most people didn't think much about the military back then and saw no reason to do so, including many members of Congress. Late in the summer of 2001, Rumsfeld was on Capitol Hill again to advocate transforming the military to meet the unconventional challenges we faced. From his confirmation hearing and through the year, he consistently pushed similar themes and objectives: The world in which we find ourselves has changed dramatically. It's less likely we'll face major armies, navies, and air forces. It's more likely we'll face asymmetrical threats, like ballistic missiles or terrorism or cyberterrorism.

"We're not organized properly for those kind of threats," he'd repeat, as he pushed the necessary but painful case for transformation.

In that congressional appearance, he sounded those themes and challenges—forcefully. Some listened, some didn't. Few gave rousing endorsements of his advocacy for dramatic change. They didn't exactly pat him on the head and say, "That's nice," before they got to their real concerns—how many ships in their backyards, how many widgets would be built—but they came close.

Not surprisingly, Rumsfeld was frustrated. Walking to his car later, he pounded his fist into his hand and said (to no one in particular, but one of his security guys and I were the only ones nearby), "Why don't they get it? Why don't they realize how important this is?"

Having worked for Rumsfeld just a few months at this point, I thought that when a secretary of defense asks a question, you answer it. Fortunately for me, in this case, I actually knew the sad answer.

"I'm the closest thing you have to an 'average American' in the Pentagon right now, sir, and I know what it's like for them and for their constituents. Most of us have gotten up for the last ten to twelve years in relative peace and prosperity. We don't know much about what's going on, about what kind of threats are growing out there. It's hard for us to imagine that something terrible could happen."

Rumsfeld stopped and turned. He looked at me for a second and then said, "Unfortunately, someday I'll be right."

Unfortunately for all of us, most people pre-9/11 were like those members of Congress. Our outreach efforts—with a few notable exceptions—met with a polite "We'll call you when there's something going on."

Just a few weeks later, everything changed. All of a sudden—

post-9/11—everybody wanted to know everything about the military. They needed to know what their military was doing and how it was accomplishing its goals. Our outreach job got easier in some respects and more challenging in others. Now we needed to prioritize diverse constituencies we wanted to reach and fight for time on a very busy schedule.

But we threw the net wide. Of course, we talked with the national security experts and retired military analysts. As importantly, we also reached out to businesses, Middle East experts, women's organizations, human rights organizations, and numerous humanitarian organizations.

Combat operations in Afghanistan started on October 7, 2001. Not long after that, I remembered our Bishops for Fast Track at USTR. I was obsessed with reaching out to people who were, in turn, reaching out to thousands and millions on a regular basis. Again, I seldom was in the pews on Sundays, but I knew that people in churches and synagogues and mosques nationwide talked about 9/11, al Qaeda, and the war on terror almost every day.

Brent Krueger, who had worked for me at USTR, headed up our Pentagon outreach efforts. He did a wonderful job under tough circumstances. The task often fell to him to explain to a two-star's aide why his boss had to spend an hour talking with educational leaders at the busiest time of his career. He always had to balance the competing groups, soothe the hurt feelings of those not invited, and withstand my never-ending demand for more information, more meetings, and more "unusual suspects" at the Pentagon.

The first time I mentioned to him the idea of asking religious leaders in, he gave me the "this one might be a bridge too far" look. The more we talked, though, the more he warmed up to the idea. And being one of the best nonsoldier soldiers in the place, he tackled the thankless task of deciding which groups and which leaders to invite.

The first meeting was in late November of 2001. We had rabbis, we had priests, we had imams and reverends. It looked like an ecumenical Noah's ark. Brent, careful not to offend any faith by seemingly "picking" one leader, invited at least two from each.

All our outreach meetings were interesting and useful. The religious leaders' meetings were fascinating. Most of them were extremely well educated, well traveled, and absolutely committed—as we were—to helping their constituencies understand the war on terror. Many of them believed, as we did, passionately, that it was important for people to understand that ours was not a war about one ethnic group or a religion. In our meetings, they were focused and energized.

Our outreach meetings generally followed a set pattern. The Joint Staff would provide a flag officer to conduct an operations briefing. A senior civilian from the policy shop would brief participants on their agenda; often General Richard Myers or then Vice Chairman of the Joint Chiefs General Peter Pace would speak as well. Each briefer always saved the bulk of his time for questions and discussion, and there always was a lot of it.

Each outreach meeting ended with Rumsfeld's spending anywhere from thirty to sixty minutes with the group. That seems like a lot of time, and it is. On a normal day, it's hard to get thirty minutes of a SecDef's time. These were not normal days. But the secretary understood and appreciated the value of the outreach. He felt an obligation, to be sure, to try to keep people informed. But he also knew he often learned something from the exchanges and benefited from the diverse views offered up during the discussions.

One of the most poignant moments came in an early meeting of the religious leaders. The discussion centered on Afghanistan but broadened to include the spread of terrorism globally—where terrorists come from and what inspires them to such fanaticism. "What are we to do when entire generations of people have decided dying is better than living?" one Baptist minister asked sadly. Nobody had an answer, but I don't think he expected one.

Cardinal Theodore E. McCarrick, the archbishop of Washington, attended a couple of our outreach meetings. Always thoughtful, he often addressed the hard, tactical matters rather than what you might consider the "spiritual" side of war. At the end of one outreach meeting, as the secretary walked around the conference room, thanking people for their participation, McCarrick motioned me over. "I have something I need to tell you and the secretary," he said. The secretary was headed our way anyhow. When he reached us, McCarrick held my hand and the secretary's. "I've seen you on TV," he said to me, "and I know what you're going through," he said to the secretary. "I want you to know I'm praying for both of you." The secretary, gracious as ever, thanked him. I mumbled something and wondered if everyone thought my briefings were so bad we needed divine intervention.

Some people may read this and say, "What a waste of time. Why should a secretary of defense spend time with people not critical to the core business?"

The answer is simple: Because these people both hear and

influence other people's opinions. Because any organization of any size—public or private—needs a wide base of support from which it can operate. Think of a house. A more solid foundation supports a larger house. It's always nice to have broadbased support; it's increasingly critical to success when just about every organization will face challenges of some kind. And when the going gets tough, often you can't count on just the usual suspects. It's not enough. Worse, they might desert you just when it's roughest.

Just as you apply out-of-the-box thinking to your audiences, you have to apply it to your communications tactics. Especially these days, conventional will only get you so far. Too many people think of effective communications as a one-way street. Get your point across, they believe, and you've succeeded. I can be as guilty of this conventional thinking as anyone else. And sometimes it takes someone out of the communications business to set me straight.

In late 2002, I was struggling—as many were—with global opinion of the United States, particularly in the Arab world. "Why Do They Hate Us?" was a common headline, and the government's episodic if well-meaning efforts to improve our image abroad weren't going far. When we did try to tell people overseas who we were and what we believed, nobody, it seemed, was listening.

We used all the standard tactics to reach out, as well as a few unconventional ones. We put op-eds in Arab papers and senior administration officials on Al Jazeera, Middle East Broadcasting, and Al Arabiya TV. We regularly courted Arab media and opinion leaders through briefings, mailings, and e-mail alerts. We did more than any of our predecessors, but it was never enough.

The more I dug into the challenge, the more I thought there was little hope in reaching many Arab adults. They watched what they watched and believed what they wanted to believe. Our chances of changing their views of the United States were slim, so I began to focus on Arab youth. Maybe, just maybe, if we could get to them before their views were hardened, we'd have more success, I thought.

Knowing little about how to reach this constituency, I reached out to people who did. There are dozens of multinational corporations that have successfully sold their products in the Arab world, despite policy differences and oft-stated anti-Americanism. So I called friends and former colleagues at companies like Disney and Ford, Microsoft and McDonald's.

"How do you do it?" I asked them all. "How do you sell something from a country perceived by many in that part of the world as anathema?" I half expected many of them to tell me they low-keyed their brand and their country of origin or that they sold their products under a different name.

Their answers were surprising and simple. "We don't promise more than we can deliver, and we deliver what we promise," one corporate exec told me about selling his product in the Middle East. "If we say we're going to open two plants in eighteen months, we make darn sure we do it," he said. "Credibility is everything in a country that inherently distrusts many Americans."

"Our physical presence is about more than our own outlets," another one told me. "We make sure we contribute to the construction of libraries and parks in key communities. People appreciate the gesture, and there's a visible, tangible sign of our commitment to them."

It's an interesting point. At the very time people around the world need to see and hear more from Americans, the primary symbol of our government—our embassies—have become fortresses with necessary yet intimidating security. Our embassy staff travel less and less frequently from their desks, much less out of capitals. The "visible, tangible" signs of commitment by the U.S. government are fewer and fewer. The ones that do exist often look more like maximum security prisons than embassies. I understand the security concerns, especially in the wake of 9/11, but such appearances aggravate tensions.

My friend Admiral "T" McCreary served in Bahrain when the United States Information Agency still existed. An agency within the Department of State, USIA had several thousand people worldwide focused on a wide range of programs to explain and support American foreign policy. It used educational, cultural, and information programs—many of them focused on in-country news media—to promote U.S. interests through greater international understanding about our country, its goals and policies.

Like any government agency, the USIA had its faults. But at the end of the day, it had our people on the streets, in the schools and civic organizations of dozens of countries, some friendly and some not so friendly. "At least," as "T" would tell me when we chewed over the problems of international opinion, "we were engaged. At least we were trying."

The Foreign Affairs and Restructuring Act abolished the USIA in October of 1999. It was a mistake then, and the long-term effects are felt keenly every day as we struggle with a better way forward with Arab opinion in particular and international views of the United States in general.

Ironically, many of the people in Washington who supported USIA's shutdown now cry loudest for new programs with the same intent as USIA had—to increase and improve international understanding. One former Jesse Helms staffer even acknowledged—okay, after several beers at a Georgetown bar—that killing USIA was a mistake. One agency does not make all the difference in how the U.S. government is perceived abroad, but it was symbolically important—both for those who wanted to kill it in the first place and those who didn't fight hard enough to save it. Looking back, its demise manifested two views at the time. One was close to isolationist, the other naïve.

My calls to corporate reps were helpful but not completely satisfying, especially when it came to my personal goal of finding ways to reach Arab youth in particular. Realizing that American music—more than just about any other domestic product—did well in the Arab world, I started digging for the expert on that sector.

My friend Hilary Rosen, then the head of the Recording Industry Association of America, got what I was looking for right away. That was no surprise. For seventeen years, several of them as president and CEO, Hilary had worked at RIAA, one of the most powerful trade associations in town. As the music industry grew, so did the challenges for RIAA. Piracy, long a concern in the entertainment world, grew exponentially, as technology advanced and made illegal downloads second nature to many. Instead of thousands of bad copies made and distributed piecemeal, the wonders of the Internet allowed millions of people to illegally download songs every day, depriving companies and artists of their rightful compensation. Hilary represented her member companies well and gracefully withstood the vigorous—and sometimes nasty—opposition from alleged consumer advocates and illegal downloaders.

Hilary always had good advice, a rare commodity in Washington, and constructive recommendations, rarer still. "You need somebody who knows that part of the world, knows music, and wouldn't be freaked out by talking to someone in the government," she said when I called her with my quest. "You need to talk to Miles Copeland."

Music aficionados will recognize the name immediately. As many people know, Miles became a rock legend as the manager of Sting and the Police. More interesting to me in the spring of 2002 was that Miles was the largest developer and distributor of Arab music in the western world. His expertise in that part of the world came naturally. Miles was the son of Miles Copeland Jr., trumpet player in the Glenn Miller Band and legendary OSS spy who helped form the CIA after World War II. Miles grew up in the Middle East, spoke Arabic fluently, and knew that part of the world well.

When I left a message in his office that Hilary Rosen suggested I call him, Miles phoned back right away. Although I never discussed his views on U.S. national security, my gut tells me he probably had some contrary opinions. Despite that, he immediately offered to fly to Washington (at his own expense) and help me kick around my problem. When Miles walked into my Pentagon office, two things became apparent immediately. First, this was not your typical Pentagon visitor. Wearing all black and sporting blondish hair below his collar, Miles got more than a few curious glances from reporters roaming the halls and offices. Secondly, after just a few minutes of conversation, I realized Miles had a more clear-eyed view of the U.S.–Middle East relationship than anyone I had heard from in years. An apologist for no one, Miles has a deep-seated sense of public responsibility and sensitivity to the potential implications of growing conflict between the United States and the Arab world.

Miles listened patiently as I launched into a description of our efforts—feeble, I admitted—to help people "understand us better." And then he diplomatically showed me how wrong I was in my thinking.

"Let me ask you something," he said. "Say a new person moves into your neighborhood. And he comes over to your house to introduce himself. You nicely invite him in, and then he proceeds to spend the next half hour talking about himself. How do you feel?"

"I feel like he really doesn't care about me," I said.

"Exactly," Miles said, banging his hand on the large conference table in my room. "It's not good enough to explain *yourself*. You have to make sure people know you're interested in them, in their lives and experiences." Miles then spent another hour with me, giving me examples of lost opportunities to increase *two-way* understanding and appreciation. "Young Arab people in particular," he said, "think no one in the U.S. likes their musicians or entertainers. That's not true, and increasingly there are Arab performers doing exceedingly well in the U.S. and the Arab world. But those Arab youth don't know that. No one has told them."

The advice was invaluable in and of itself. Like our mutual friend Hilary, though, Miles had constructive suggestions. One recommendation should have been easy to execute: take a half-dozen Arab performers and send them on a tour of the United States and Europe. Film and document everything, including the robust crowds, the positive media coverage. Turn that into a documentary you then show and promote in the Arab world.

"Think about the headlines in the Arab world," Miles said. "Sellout U.S. crowds for Arab performers. That would have a positive impact with Arab youth."

One idea, admittedly, but a good one. And one that wouldn't cost much money. Despite that, we couldn't get it done. Despite a $400 billion DOD budget, I couldn't find a legal way to fund it out of the Pentagon. Despite good friends and colleagues at State, I could not get it done there either. I kick myself to this day for not pushing harder, but I ran up against what is a growing problem with government at the federal level. There is little imagination and less tolerance for out-of-the box thinking. It's not that some people don't want to take chances or do things differently. It's just that the bureaucracy has grown to such a level, and the penalties for failure are so high, it's very hard to connect new ideas with action.

That lack of imagination—the inability to embrace outsiders—has negative implications far beyond my failure to get Miles's great idea executed. In the wake of 9/11, almost every living soul in the United States wanted to do *something*. People wanted to help. At the Pentagon we began to realize how much so many people wanted to be a part of something bigger than themselves. They sent cards and letters and money. They sent quilts made by grandmothers and kids and people with disabilities. They sent so many posters, the Pentagon's seventeen miles of corridors were crowded with colorful, heartfelt expressions of sorrow and support. One person sent a coconut painted red, white, and blue. A school sent about thirty thousand American flag pins made of the tiniest red, white, and blue safety pins you've ever seen.

People called and wrote offering to volunteer. The lawyers said we couldn't accept volunteers, so many offices—including mine—hired contractors to help handle the postattack crush of work. In short, everybody wanted to do *something*. And we failed them. At a historic time, we failed to give them opportunities to engage with their fellow citizens in a meaningful way. We had no imagination and little capacity to offer them much of a reply other than "Go shopping."

I thought, as many did, about World War II—about the victory gardens and the tin collecting. I have older friends and relatives who still today talk fondly about how proud they were to take part—even a small one—in an important cause. Like the maps families kept on their walls to track progress in the military operations, their sacrifices at home helped them feel as though they were part of the team.

"War bonds," I said to Di Rita's morning group one day in late September of 2001. "We ought to issue war bonds so people have some tangible sign that they're part of this war." My colleagues loved the idea, so I thought I was on to something. But our enthusiasm wasn't matched by some others in the government.

"It makes no sense financially," one Treasury bureaucrat told me emphatically when I called to make the pitch. "We thought of it, but it's not a good investment."

"It's not for financial reasons," I practically yelled as I realized this idea was going nowhere fast. "It's for morale and encouragement and patriotism."

Click.

Maybe I should have gone to a higher authority. When necessary, Secretary Rumsfeld could be the *best* action officer, for instance. Given his priorities at the time—organizing and launching our military response in Afghanistan—I thought maybe he shouldn't be bothered. I was wrong.

Either persistent or stupid, I did try again just a week later. As general manager of Hill and Knowlton's Washington office prior to my Pentagon stint, I had been fortunate enough to oversee the team that developed the U.S. Mint's highly successful "50 State Quarters" marketing program. Quickly becoming one of the most successful collectibles ever, the quarters were hugely popular with people of all ages and backgrounds. The program was clear and the rules strict: over a few years, issue a new quarter for each state in the order in which they entered the union. Despite the name of the program, I thought the extraordinary times could accommodate one exception.

Issue a one-time-only quarter called the "United in Freedom" quarter, I pleaded with a different Treasury bureaucrat. "People will have something they can hold and display and feel proud about when they use it in a store."

"We can't," the Treasury official told me. "We'd have to go to Congress and get legislation to change the Fifty State Quarters program."

"That's even better," I said. "Everyone in Congress wants to do something too. This will give them another opportunity to make a difference."

Click.

Tom Friedman of the *New York Times* writes intelligently and purposefully most of the time. One of his most poignant columns was one he wrote on December 9, 2001, called "Ask Not

What . . ." He communicated far more persuasively than I ever did with my Treasury colleagues what a unique opportunity we had to engage the American people, to pull them together despite any political differences, to make a real difference. "There is a deep hunger in America post–Sept. 11 in many people who feel this is their war in their backyard and they would like to be summoned by the president to do something more than go shopping," Friedman wrote. And he offered up specific and good suggestions.

"Imagine if tomorrow President Bush asked all Americans to turn down their home thermostats to 65 degrees so America would not be so much of a hostage to Middle East oil? Trust me, every American would turn down the thermostat to 65 degrees."

Friedman described the power of the president encouraging young Americans to participate in public service, the military or Peace Corps or Teach for America. What if every U.S. school raised money for solar-powered light bulbs for African kids who don't have electricity, Friedman asked, and went on to suggest those bulbs have American flags on them, ". . . so when those kids grew up, they would remember who lit up their nights." Friedman was right, and we made a big mistake in not seizing an amazing—probably once-in-a-lifetime—opportunity.

Not every opportunity is once-in-a-lifetime. But competition in the information arena is so intense, you have to pursue every opportunity, large and small. That's what made me think of cartoons as one part of a strategy.

Secretary Rumsfeld loves editorial cartoons. He'd deny it, but his affection for them borders on obsession. Throughout his long career, he has collected originals of cartoonists from around the world who use creative drawing to praise, prod, and (attempt to) provoke him. Sometimes, I thought, the tougher the cartoon, the more he got a kick out of it.

His focus on them got me thinking about editorial cartoons and their reach. Like many visual images, editorial cartoons did stick in people's minds, sometimes longer than written editorials. So we added editorial cartoonists to our ever-growing outreach lists and did our best to reach their fans through their cartoons.

Sometimes we failed—like the time I agreed to address the Washington convention of the American Association of Editorial Cartoonists. Most of them appreciated that I used (with permission) many of their cartoons in my remarks. But one guy was so bent on arguing with me about whether or not the U.S. military did enough in combat to protect journalists that we all got a little cranky at the event.

Mike Luckovich of the *Atlanta Constitution-Journal* was a different story. Mike's a Pulitzer Prize winner and heck of a nice guy; we first met when Rumsfeld traveled to Atlanta for events that included an editorial board meeting with Mike's paper.

In early '03, as preparations for a potential war with Iraq heated up, Mike had done a couple of cartoons featuring the secretary. Anticipating that the secretary would want copies, my military assistant, Major Riccoh Player, called Luckovich to make the request. The conversation went something like this:

Mike: Hello?
Riccoh: Hello, sir. My name is Major Riccoh Player, and I
am calling from Public Affairs at the Pentagon.

> *Mike: Who is this?*
> *Riccoh: Major Riccoh Player from the Pentagon, sir.*
> *Mike: Your name is* Major Player?
> *Riccoh: Yes sir. (Riccoh is now rolling his eyes, since he has*
> *heard something like this about once a day since he*
> *became a major.)*
> *Mike: The Pentagon has a* Major Player?
> *Riccoh: Yes sir, and may I tell you why I'm calling?*
> *Mike: This is great! I know a* Major Player *at the*
> *Pentagon!*

And a wonderful friendship was started. As Riccoh entertained us with his version of the story (I am sure Mike's is a *little* different), I had an idea. "Why don't you invite him up?" I said to Riccoh. "National Geographic did a documentary called 'Inside the Pentagon,' C-SPAN did a 'Day in the Life of the Pentagon.' He can do an editorial cartoonist's 'Day at the Pentagon.'"

Since you seldom know what might happen on any given day at the Pentagon, it was a bit of a gamble, but one we thought worth taking. I am not sure where the whole idea of a one-armed push-up contest between Riccoh and Mike started, but it was just one highlight of what turned out to be a busy day for Mike and a good day for our use of an alternative means of communication.

As luck would have it, David Hume Kennerly, the extraordinary photographer and a Rumsfeld friend, happened to be in the building that day too. Actually, luck had nothing to do with it. Kennerly was often in the building, capturing some exceptional images of a Pentagon at war.

He captured the one-arm push-up contest that day. Mike says he won by six push-ups. "Short cartoonists are often underestimated," he recounted in the *Atlanta Constitution-Journal,* but I'm pretty sure Riccoh let him win.

Mike captured the "surprise" visit by the president that day to meet with the service chiefs, as well as the SecDef's outreach lunch meeting with the "formers," as we called them, people like Kissinger and Albright and Schlesinger.

"They were hard to draw," Mike wrote in his full-page spread in his paper, "because they were all chewing."

The combination of Mike's good nature, the access we gave him, and the events of the day combined to make the "bit of a gamble" a home run. Mike turned his day (and Kennerly's photos) into a full-page, first-person account/cartoon/photo montage. As if that weren't enough, Atlanta-based CNN put him on air a few days later to share his story with Aaron Brown. Not bad—and a way of reaching people whom we couldn't have reached through traditional media vehicles alone.

Every situation described above is unique, but the lessons are constant:

- Know the direct route is not always the best way to get somewhere.
- Be willing to take chances. Not every gamble pays off, but a forward leaning approach is the best one.
- If you can't think outside the box, be willing to embrace people who can.

So often, communication tools aren't always words or images. They're actions too. To survive in today's information era, you need to employ multiple tools. To *succeed*, you have to be very creative in how you do it. And, of course, you have to be creative about solving problems too.

In June of 2002, we headed off with Rumsfeld on a multi-nation tour that would include stops in India and Pakistan at a time of extremely high tension between the two nations. We covered ten countries in ten days, a whirlwind but typical trip for Rumsfeld, who wasted no time—ever. Gallows humor was rampant throughout the trip. It didn't take the traveling press tour long to dub it "Rumsfeld's No Nukes Tour." And it took no time at all when we got home for the T-shirts to be printed up, complete with the list of the stops on our "tour" listed down the back.

Also typical of Rumsfeld was the small staff with which he traveled and on whom he depended to pull together the myriad details that go into travel of a major cabinet secretary. While most cabinet officers have handfuls—if not dozens—of advance people, we had two, for the entire Department of Defense. Ever mindful of the taxpayers' dollars, Rumsfeld insisted we keep all expenses to a minimum, so complex, multination advance work fell to two young men, Chris Harvin and Bill Turenne. Young and with tons of energy—thank God—Chris and Bill would hopscotch around the country and world, flying coach, seldom sleeping in the same town two nights in a row.

Fortunately for all of us, Bill and Chris didn't know how overworked, underpaid, and poorly resourced they were. They never said "can't" and never complained. They did their jobs extraordinarily well. The No Nukes tour was typical in terms of time constraints and competing interests. The stakes were a little higher, though, as the India-Pakistan tension was intense and the public scrutiny of Rumsfeld's visits to the two countries even higher than usual. Logistics were never easy in those two countries, but India this time posed some special challenges, and Chris encountered them all as he set things up for our arrival. Schedules shifted, security was a huge concern, and there was the ever-present (polite) arguing with embassy and Indian Defense Ministry staff over meeting participants and media coverage.

The highlight—if it could be called that—of the visit to Delhi would be an outdoor press conference for Rumsfeld and his Indian counterpart, Defense Minister George Fernandes, to be held in the courtyard outside the Defense Ministry. The obvious concern was security; it was an open space with major roads nearby. The heat would be intense, in the nineties, with no shade in sight. Having experienced similar issues before, Chris doggedly worked through them, one by one. And then a new one popped up.

Monkeys. Dozens of them. Running, squealing, hissing, and spitting all over the very spot where the next day Rumsfeld and his counterpart would proclaim the strength of the U.S.–Indian military relationship and stress the importance of lowering tensions with neighboring Pakistan. Only no one would be able to see or hear them over the hordes of monkeys. Harvin and his Indian counterparts—usually in a ratio of one to about twenty— got to work chasing the monkeys out of the courtyard. For most of them, yelling and stomping did the trick. If you saw Chris in an adrenaline- and coffee-fueled state, you would run too.

Unless you were this one monkey. About three and a half feet high at the shoulder, this fellow was not impressed with Chris and had no intention of leaving his courtyard, defense ministers or no defense ministers. Yelling didn't work, banging on pots didn't help, and a carefully fired shot or two had little impact. As a matter of fact, the big guy, not surprisingly, was getting ticked off by the noise and motion and became even more aggressive. The obvious nightmare scenario flashed through Chris's advance-man brain—a huge howling and spitting monkey disrupting the secretary's press conference, scheduled for the next morning. Not good. Determined not to be the first U.S. advance man on whose watch a monkey attacks the SecDef, Harvin got to work.

He looked for a monkey expert. What he found was an Indian translator at the U.S. Embassy who seemed to know more about monkeys than his counterparts with the Defense Ministry. He told Chris to upgrade. More specifically, he told him it was time to get a bigger monkey, one that could intimidate the local beast. Spending his own money, which often happened, Chris found somebody who knew somebody in the neighborhood who had a monkey—a really big one.

All it took was one walk around the courtyard with the four-foot monkey for the former king of the courtyard to skulk off, never to be seen again. We didn't see him the next day during the meetings, and he didn't show up at the press conference. Just to be on the safe side, Chris had his new furry friend walked around the perimeter of the courtyard until the press conference was over and the SecDef's motorcade had cleared the grounds.

The lesson? Even in communications, size does matter.

CHAPTER 5

Isn't That Why We Hired You?

*In the Information Age,
everyone's a communicator.*

I don't mind paying four bucks for coffee at Starbucks. Really, I don't. Just to irritate them, I do ask for "small, medium, and large" rather than "tall, grande, and venti." But the money doesn't bother me, at least on most days. And I'll tell you why.

Nine years ago, just when Starbucks was really taking over the world, there was a terrible tragedy at their store in the Washington, D.C., neighborhood of Georgetown. Three young employees were brutally murdered—shot several times and left to die sometime after the store closed. Another employee arrived at work the next morning and found their bodies.

Even in Washington, once the murder capital of the country, the slayings shocked the town. One factor was the location. Few murders happen in tony Georgetown, especially the heavily trafficked area on Wisconsin Avenue where this store was located. Another was the victims themselves. They were young: two were twenty-five years old and one was just eighteen. They were well-known and liked by friends and customers.

If the Starbucks corporate division had wanted to simply issue a statement and conduct their affairs with the families and the law enforcement personnel privately, I think most people would have understood. Instead, Chairman and CEO Howard Schultz took the exact opposite approach. He left his vacation and flew by chartered jet straight to Washington. Within hours of the murders, he met with the families, talked with the Georgetown employees, and pledged his and the company's commitment to help find the murderers and memorialize the lives lost. He didn't send a deputy. He didn't act through lawyers in town—although I'm sure some people, worried about the company's liability, recommended that. When it came to the worst thing that had happened since he joined Starbucks in 1982, he handled the major activities—internal and external—himself.

That alone would distinguish Schultz from most CEOs. But he took his responsibilities even further. He met with the media frequently. He pledged his commitment to help find the murderers—Starbucks offered a $100,000 reward—and stayed in close contact with the victims' families and the other employees at the store as the days and weeks went by.

Just ten days after the murders, Schultz attended a memorial service for the slain workers at Georgetown University's Gaston Hall. Many people had wondered what would happen to the store where the murders occurred, and Schultz didn't take long to figure it out. After the memorial service, attended by over one thousand friends and families and scores of media, Schultz announced that the store would be reopened with all future profits going to an antiviolence organization.

"We stand here powerless to reverse the tragedy of last week and incapable of mending the hearts of our 23,000 partners, who so personally feel the emptiness left by our fallen partners' death," Schultz was quoted in a *Washington Post* story. "But by dedicating the remodeled store in their honor, and by contributing all future net profits from sales at the Georgetown store, we hope to keep their spirits alive."

Schultz realized what a lot of executives don't: especially at a critical time, communications was a key part of his responsibility as CEO. Rumsfeld did too. In the early months after the war in Afghanistan started, we had Rumsfeld, the Chairman of the Joint Chiefs General Richard Myers, and other senior leadership out early and often in the briefing room. America was in a very different kind of war, and it was important for us to try to explain it to the country as clearly and consistently as possible.

When Rumsfeld started briefing frequently after 9/11, it became clear that, unlike most people in Washington, he speaks without the superficial gloss that covers most policy makers' statements.

U.S. News & World Report called the style "Rum Punch" in a cover article on Rumsfeld in December of 2001. "Beware the

Myers—should brief and brief frequently. They should do interviews, outreach meetings, speeches—all in an effort to provide as much news and information as possible about the military. The leaders of this country sign orders that send young men and women to fight and sometimes die in battle. They should be accountable and responsible. The men and women in uniform deserve it. Men like Rumsfeld and Myers understand that.

Leaders are just where it starts. Everyone—from the person running the company to the assistant answering the phones—is a communicator.

"Isn't that why we hired you?" one former boss asked when I suggested he should do a few interviews on an important topic. So why? Why does everyone *have* to be a communicator? Why have two or four horses in a harness rather than one? Because more can pull a heavier load. More voices are needed to break through the clutter of the information era. Secondly, it goes to credibility. Increasingly, people want their information straight from the horse's mouth, a trend that goes to the general disintermediation in society. Why do people go to Price Club or Sam's Club or buy things online? Because they don't need all the marketing and hype that often accompany retail sales. Similarly, in communications, people are suspicious of the spinners and increasingly view the news media's role with cynicism and doubt. If the topic is engineering, people want an engineer to explain it. If it's a crisis that impacts an entire organization, they want to see the CEO out front, not hiding behind corporate spokesmen.

There's a side benefit to leadership's leaning forward on communications. As they say, lead by example. Why would a busy midlevel manager take time to meet with reporters or do some local outreach? Simple. If his boss thinks it's a good use of his time, it must be worth doing. Because Rumsfeld, Myers, Pace, and other senior leadership at the Pentagon were willing to brief the news media regularly, conduct dozens of outreach sessions, and troop to Capitol Hill on a regular basis, we could convince others in the Pentagon and the U.S. military to take a similarly robust posture.

In the summer of 2001, we started a series of casual briefings intended to help the news media get to know some of the new people in the building and vice versa. New staff ranged from Craig Duehring, the principal deputy assistant secretary of defense for reserve affairs, to J. D. Crouch, assistant secretary of defense for international security policy, to Peter Rodman, assistant secretary of defense for international security affairs. Some briefings were more interesting than others, but having at least one low-key, relatively risk-free session with the media helped ease the way down the road when we asked the same people to address hot and newsworthy topics.

In the days and weeks right after 9/11, there was, not surprisingly, a lot of interest in the reconstruction of the Pentagon itself. We frequently called on Army Major General Jim Jackson, the commanding general of the Military District of Washington, who coordinated the various forces—law enforcement, labor, fire, and police. Similarly, we asked Lee Evey, the head of the renovation project, to brief so often that he became something of a rock star.

Many did not want to do the briefings. They had important jobs at a critical time, and they were working around the clock. But we were able to convince them that informing and educating people was just as critical a part of the restoration as the work being done by hundreds of construction workers. In some ways, it would have been easier for me or another regular briefer to deliver some talking points that characterized the general state of affairs. It was far more credible and helpful to have an engineer describe—in some detail—the progress being made. And someone with substantive knowledge can often bring needed perspective.

From the very instant the plane hit the Pentagon, it was important to me that people know that the terrorists had failed in their efforts to destroy the building. It was a terrible tragedy in which many people lost their lives and were injured, but the terrorists had failed. As bad as the damage to the Pentagon was, the size and strength of the building lessened the blow. Lee could make that point crystal clear—and did in his first full briefing on September 15, 2001:

> To put things in perspective for you, though, the face on each of the five sides is a bit longer than three football fields in length. It's got 42,420 columns which hold the building up, and we've lost some of those columns. But to put that loss in perspective, there's over 42,000 of them in the building. It's got 85,000 light fixtures, six and a half million square feet, seventeen and a half miles of corridors, 16,000 miles of communications cabling. It's a very, very large building.

That was a statement I couldn't have delivered—at least not as credibly as an engineer could. Lee went on to explain that the plane's main impact point was right where they had just completed renovations, renovations undertaken primarily to strengthen the building.

Now this was a terrible tragedy and people lost their lives. But I'm here to tell you that had we not undertaken this effort in the building, this could have been much, much worse.

At a grim time, Lee's detailed assessment offered some comfort.

Leaders at headquarters are important communicators, but they're only part of the effort. Indeed, a major premise behind the embedding program in Iraq was my conviction that our troops in the field were our best spokespeople. I had less confidence that the public affairs officers (PAOs) who would escort the embedded reporters during actual combat shared my convictions. We had recruited Jim Wilkinson from the White House Press Office to head Strategic Communications for Central Command. Jim headed to Tampa in late 2002 just as planning for a potential war with Iraq was ramping up. He heard me say repeatedly that we needed truly exceptional people in those PAO slots. They would come under his supervision to a large extent, and I wanted to make sure he took a hard look at the personnel choices. "T" did the bulk of the heavy lifting on this front, negotiating, arm twisting, and cajoling the services into sending forward some of their best people.

I made the importance clear, but I didn't convey the mission and intent to Jim.

"We have terrific people," he said happily. "They have tons of experience working with the media, they're all comfortable on camera, and they will be great spokesmen in the field."

I realized my mistake immediately. "We don't need terrific spokesmen," I said. "The best spokesmen *and* spokeswomen will be those kids in uniform doing the hard work under extraordinary circumstances. We want them out there with the media, not some flacks. And if it's not the kids, it's the unit commander or the closest flag officer, on camera, giving some perspective to what's going on." Getting that done would require a very different kind of public affairs officer.

"We need people who aren't afraid to push the edge of the envelope," I said. "People who will stand up to their boss and advocate what we've said we're going to do—facilitate robust media coverage of the war. I want the guy who's willing to stand up to a two-star or three-star and say, 'This is the way we have to do it.'"

To ensure everyone understood what I failed to communicate to Jim, we held a series of video teleconferences (VTCs) with the PAOs who would be in the field. There was no way we could micromanage such a mammoth effort from Washington, I knew, and we would have to trust people to make the best decision at the "local" level. By making clear, again and again, the goals of embedding and the principles on which we would base all actions, I knew they would make the right decisions.

The people I described to Jim are hard to find, but "T" and his team found them. Most of the PAOs became fierce advocates for their embedded journalists, some stretching the rules so far, I am glad I never heard about it until well after the fact. They understood the mission and intent, and they executed it superbly.

Your employees—at all levels—can and should act as force multipliers, communicating the company's overarching goals. You want them to stay in their lanes, but you also want them out there—whether it's with fellow employees, the local Chamber of Commerce, or the news media—spreading the good news when there is some and dispelling rumors and misinformation when it's out there. Keep them in the dark, and you'll have nothing but problems. Keep them informed, make clear you think communications is part of their jobs, and they'll thrive and add real value to your company.

For the U.S. Marine Corps, that approach is second nature. I was working at Bozell-Eskew, the issues advocacy advertising agency, when then Secretary of Defense William S. Cohen asked us to study the military's recruiting marketing campaigns and make recommendations. It was the late '90s, jobs were plentiful, and the military was concerned about meeting its numbers for the all-volunteer force.

Janet Langhart Cohen, the secretary's wife and a former television newscaster, was the first to explain the problem to the secretary. The services were trying to reach kids in their late teens to early twenties. If you turned on CBS on a Sunday night, you'd likely see recruiting ads on *60 Minutes*. The median age for *60 Minutes* viewers is about the same as its name—sixty! Not quite the target audience.

The issues were complex, but the crux of the matter was obvious: the services were looking in the wrong places and using the wrong tools to reach their target audiences. It didn't take long in our study—several months and dozens of interviews with everyone from the senior brass on down to recent recruits—to learn something else. Recruiting for the Army, Navy, and Air Force was a distinct role and responsibility for one segment of each service. There was little coordination—or even contact—between the recruiting staff and anyone else in the service. That's a slight oversimplification, but not by much.

I asked a lead recruiter for one service, "What do you do

with the public affairs staff and communications people? If your service secretary has said that improving recruiting is a priority, what do they bring to the table?" He didn't pause a beat. "We have no contact with them." Public affairs staff didn't see recruiting as their responsibility; neither did many others in the services outside the recruiting command.

His answer said volumes, and the Marines were living proof of the benefits of their very different approach. Partly because of their size, much smaller than the other services, the Marines have always been good at shining a spotlight on their accomplishments, high standards, and tough requirements. Not everybody is right for the Marines, and they are rightfully proud of that distinction. But everyone in the Marines knows that he or she is responsible for recruiting more of the right kind of people into the Corps. Every last one of them is a communicator. As the saying goes, "Once a Marine, always a Marine," and Marines carry that pride throughout life. They take their mission to recruit very seriously, no matter what their core responsibilities might be.

By the end of our study and myriad briefings to recruiting commands and Pentagon briefings, there was one standard and all-important talking point: With the Marines, from the commandant in Washington, D.C., to the guy pumping gas at Quantico, everyone knows that part of his responsibility is recruiting. And every one of them lives it every day.

Some recruiters in other services discount the Marines' success and chalk it up to the fact that they don't need as many recruits. I disagree. They work hard at it—very hard. Just as important, they take seriously the idea that everyone—from the commandant down to the private—has responsibility to communicate one of the Corps' major missions.

Carla Hills understood that concept. During her time at USTR, you could grab anybody from the guard at the front desk to any of the negotiators to the interns in the attic, and they could all articulate the key messages: "Our mission is to open markets and expand trade. We'll work within multilateral organizations whenever possible and employ unilateral tools when absolutely necessary." Each person could then go on to explain his role in achieving that mission. I think you could drag people who worked at USTR back then out of a dead sleep, ask them what the mission was, and get exactly that answer today. And despite very tough jobs that often entailed much travel, USTR staff willingly spoke to different public groups, traveled to and from Capitol Hill on a regular basis, and patiently answered scores of questions from an aggressive press corps.

One of the more enjoyable aspects of my Pentagon life—and one I continue today—is participation in the Capstone program, an intense training and orientation for what I called the "baby brass," those select few officers who have just received their first star. No disrespect intended with my nickname for them, by the way. Most of them think they're hot stuff, and in the military hierarchy, they are. More to the point, some of them think that once they've gotten to this level, there are certain things they won't have to do. They have more people reporting to them and perhaps, just perhaps, they can delegate some of the most onerous tasks—for example, dealing with the media, the Congress, or even just the general public. There are exceptions—increasingly, military leaders recognize the role of information in their business—but there are still many who think their responsibility for communications, at best, is to get good people in those jobs.

When I do a Capstone presentation, the most interesting part is always the discussion and Q&A afterwards. The topics are diverse, but one question often gets asked: "Can you help us figure out where to find the right kind of public affairs people? And how can we get them the best training?" The officers are well-intentioned, I know, but their concern is misguided, and I always tell them so.

"I'd worry less about that," I say, "and more about *your* role in all this." Their faces show confusion and—among those who know where I am headed with that lead—some disappointment. "Being able to communicate what you are doing and how you're getting there is a primary responsibility for you—not just some people down the chain of command. You have a leadership task. Ensure that those who work for you embrace communications as an integral part of your overall operations. And you have to 'lead from the front,' as they say in the military. Do it yourself."

My sessions usually end pretty quickly after that.

The era in which one person or office could carry the communications load for an organization is over. In its place are increased responsibilities:

- Everyone from front line troops to senior management has a role in communications. Employ them all properly, and you will have a tremendous force multiplier.
- Lead from the front. To ensure participation and the integration necessary for a communications program to succeed, an organization's head has to demonstrate through word and deed that he understands the impact of communications on the bottom line. Do the interviews, give the speeches, and others will follow.

CHAPTER 6

Communications
Is a Science, Not an Art

*Have clearly defined objectives, strategies,
and tactics—ones that drive the bottom line.*

Most people think of communications as an art. It's a convenient construction, because what it basically means is that you don't have to work hard at it, pay attention to detail, and reach into the nitty-gritty of managing people and getting things done. The truth is dramatically different. Communications isn't an art. It's a science—not rocket science, mind you, but a rigorous, detailed, painstaking endeavor that requires organization and discipline to be successful.

Approach communications as an add-on to your operations, and you will fail in the information era. Elevate communications, apply the same intense planning, resourcing, and measurements to it as to core operations, and you succeed. In the private sector, there are countless examples of organizations that saw communications as the "extra" to be considered only when the media called or a crisis had already occurred. I doubt the executives at Enron shared their accounting schemes with their communications staffs—even though any communications pro might have avoided the whole crisis with one question: "How are you going to feel when that scheme appears in the newspaper?"

On the flip side, some of the most successful companies today have highly integrated communications programs that recognize information's vital role and give the communications staff the right support and clout. Although many things contribute to successful communications, at the end of the day, it comes down to people, planning, and integration.

Start with the obvious: your people. Hire communications staff with significant experience in a wide range of communications functions. That might be journalism, public relations, or government, but pay what it takes to get good people. More importantly, put them at the grown-ups' table. In title and deed, demonstrate to the entire organization that the senior communications official is just as relevant as the chief of operations or the general counsel or the head of IT.

And the senior communications staff should be able to build comprehensive plans that address short- and long-term objectives for the company. Different organizations have different names for planning. Some in the military use "SMEAC," which stands for "situation, mission, execution, administration, and communication." They start with the environment in which they find themselves (the situation), they make clear they know what they're to do (mission), they develop a strategy (execution), figure out what it will take resourcewise to execute the plan (administration), and they make darn sure everyone involved knows what the plan is (communication). It's a great discipline for planning a military operation, and it's equally useful in building and executing a communications program. It's exactly what we did in building the embedding plan for the Iraq war, and it had several benefits. First, the discipline helped us build a very strong program. Second, the very fact that we used a system applied most often to military operations increased the comfort level of some in uniform who were understandably reluctant about putting reporters on the front lines.

The problem is, most people have plans for what they consider the substantive side of a business or organization; they don't apply the same approach to communications, and that's a mistake. Whatever the name, every significant communications operation should have rigorous standards applied to it. What's the mission, the clearly defined objectives? Next, what's the strategy? Then, what tools and tactics will you use?

Getting a positive article in the *New York Times* is not a strategy. It's a means to an end, perhaps, but not a strategy. Unless you've got a goal to accomplish, a story in the *New York Times* is just something to do. (Warning: public relations firms that bill by the hour *love* things to do.)

In the late '90s many of the major health care insurers were under heat for a host of reasons. The executives of one firm that was facing multiple lawsuits and potential congressional scrutiny asked me, "How can you help us?" Typical for me, I answered with a question: "What do you want to accomplish?" The CEO immediately launched into complaints about specific articles in the media over the past few months and said, "We need a really big front-page article in the *Wall Street Journal!*"

There were two problems. First, CEOs rarely make it onto the front page of the *Wall Street Journal* for anything positive. Second, he didn't seem to have any idea what that article would say or how it would help his company. Not surprisingly, he didn't appreciate my joke that most CEOs on the front page had the word "embattled" close by.

"You tell me what you want to accomplish *substantively,* and I'll build you the right communications program," I said. That sounds simple, but defining an organization's goals can be quite difficult, whether it's what kind of widget they're building or what they want to have happen on the policy front. And the dirty little secret is that communications problems often have less to do with communications and more to do with that basic inability to define core objectives.

So any communications program needs some basic elements:

Objectives—"Generating positive media coverage" is not an objective. It may help accomplish your goals, but positive coverage for positive coverage's sake isn't that valuable. Does the coverage drive the bottom line? *That's* positive coverage. True objectives might be: Raise awareness among soccer moms about Ford SUV safety features. Create a more favorable environment in which Congress views the cable TV industry. Neutralize the impact of al Qaeda disinformation in the Arab world.

Strategy—You need a game plan that makes clear *how* you will achieve your communications objectives. Just as "We're going to put points on the board" is not a strategy for a football coach, outreach to consumer media is not a strategy to increase awareness among policy makers of Tylenol child safety measures. It may be one part of your plan, but it's not a strategy.

As discussed before, the objectives behind the embedding program were to build and maintain support for our troops and deter or neutralize Iraqi regime disinformation and deception tactics. The strategy was equally simple: Achieve information dominance. Employ as many vehicles as possible—primarily the news media—to fill as many of the information vacuums as possible with accurate information about military activities.

Prioritized Audiences—You cannot be all things to all people, so figure out on whom you want to focus your energies and to what degree. At the Pentagon, we knew we wanted to keep the "immediate family," the "formers," and the retired military and the veterans and service organizations in the loop. That required sustained action, but since they were an informed audience, the lifting wasn't so heavy. We also wanted to improve our relationships with important audiences like minorities and business organizations. Less initial awareness on their part meant sustained and heavy lifting for us much of the time. And we had groups—like women and educators—with whom we wanted to build relationships where few existed. Obviously, that meant doing lots of work and keeping our expectations firmly in check.

The word "sustained" is in there for a reason. Don't talk to somebody once and think they get whatever you're selling. At the end of the day, successful communications hinges as much on relationships as anything else, and relationships require work, persistence, and patience.

When John McCain first moved to the Senate from the House in 1987, we had more on our plate, of course, since he now represented the whole state and had a lot more interest from reporters, including the Arizona media. Anne Q. Hoy was the first-rate reporter based in Washington, D.C., for the *Arizona Republic,* the largest paper in the state. The majority of the time, we all got along with her fine. In hindsight, I think she was kind not to point out too often the many rookie mistakes I am sure we made. I don't even remember the incident that caused me to explode with Anne, but I did one day. Words were exchanged, mine more heated than Anne's, and the encounter ended with some phone slamming and my exclaiming to anyone who would listen that "we are through with her," one of those things you say every once in a while, even though there's a little voice in the back of your head saying, "You know you really can't do that, don't you?" Anyhow, John heard my rants and wandered by my desk. Remarkably, he didn't laugh right in my face. Instead, he gave me one of the better lessons of my time in Washington.

"Relationships are like bank accounts," he said. "You have to make lots of deposits, because every once in a while you have to make a big withdrawal." He then suggested that I take a day to cool off, realize I had just made a big withdrawal, and start making deposits again.

He's absolutely right. And as you prioritize your audiences and decide how and when you will address them, be realistic. Don't expect anything from people if you're not willing to make a serious commitment to them.

Tactics—Major and minor, tactics have to be developed and executed with the same discipline one would apply to assembling a complex piece of machinery. And in the world of communications, there are vast new avenues of communication above and beyond the news media. As discussed in chapter three, you must tailor the tool you use for the audience you're trying to reach.

Themes and Messages—What are the most important messages for your audiences to hear? Your goals? Your product's qualities? Your mission? That's what you want worked into every conversation and communication, no matter what the particular situation might be. Prior to 9/11, the overarching themes for the Pentagon were to transform the Department of Defense, to address asymmetrical threats, and to recruit and retain the best people for the military. Post-9/11, "asymmetrical threats" evolved into the war on terror, but the core themes have held up pretty well over time.

Measurement—As hard and tangible as the inputs ought to be in communications, the outputs are hard to measure. You have to be honest with yourself. Is the trend in media coverage positive or negative? Has the trend developed because of a concerted effort to work more closely with the media covering your sector, or despite it? If customers provide positive feedback to an e-mail alert system you developed to keep them abreast of company news, track it and report it up the food chain. Do research—legitimate research—to find out if perceptions of your organization have changed and if so, why?

Integration—Of all the elements that drive successful communications, the most important is integration. As they say, "To

help you on the landing, I need to be there at the takeoff."
Don't expect communications staff to bail you out in a disaster
if you didn't tell them where you were headed in the first place.
Include communications people in all key functions, especially
the earliest planning of significant operations, and make clear to
others in the organization that they have communications roles
and responsibilities.

If they're in the mix, the communications staff can push hard
on policy or operations people who may not have thought
through all the potential consequences of a decision. Good
communications people tend to be a paranoid lot. They can
often spot a truly awful disaster before it occurs.

And the relationship works both ways. The substantive
folks—at best having long experience with a product or issue—
can help communications. If they know their job well, they can
probably reduce it to a simple message. They offer details that
enhance a major point or add to the list of relevant audiences
and the most effective tools to reach them. Integrated correctly,
the operational types can move a communications plan from
good to superior.

There's a great litmus test for successful, integrated communications. Randomly pull ten people out of an organization and
ask each of them, "What do you do here?" In most cases, you'll
get a variety of answers. In a truly successful program, everyone
from the security guard up to the CEO can state what the overarching mission is and what role he or she plays in that mission.
The classic example is NASA in the 1960s. There, everyone
from the top scientists down to the cleaning crew understood
the mission—put a man on the moon in ten years. Pull a scien-
tist from his NASA lab in 1965 and ask him what his job was,

and he'd answer, "I'm putting a man on the moon," and follow up with a concise statement on his role in that mission. Pull a janitor off his cleaning duties at three a.m. at Cape Canaveral and ask him the same question. His answer: "I'm putting a man on the moon," followed by how his rigorous cleaning of the facilities helped ensure flawless operations in the labs.

They all got it. They knew what the mission was and what their role in it was. That should be the goal for every organization.

Building a truly effective communications program requires a willingness to take a long-term approach. Issues, crises, and events always pop up—usually when you least expect or want them to. How effectively you handle them depends almost completely on your organization's ongoing work. The ability to absorb a blow and keep moving forward hinges on how well you've done your job in the preceding months and years.

I tend to think better visually. And I see effective communications as a three-tiered pyramid. It goes from the widest but easiest effort at the bottom to the narrowest but most intense effort at the top.

The base, the widest part of the pyramid, is the foundation. That's where you build and maintain support and appreciation for your organization with a broad range of constituents. In a cable company, this level might be about communicating your improved service or advanced technologies. With educators and parents, it might be about wiring schools and libraries with free high-speed Internet access. With Wall Street, it might be about the rapid growth in programming choices offered and the rising number of high-speed Internet customers. These are the fundamentals from which you advance your agenda.

The next level up—the center of the pyramid, a little bit narrower—is advocacy. What are you pushing from a policy or business perspective? What are you for or against on fundamental issues? If you're the American Medical Association (AMA), one plank is advocating reduced liability for doctors. At the Pentagon, overhauling the personnel system is one major initiative. At a private sector company, it might be increasing market share in emerging markets.

At the top, the narrowest yet most intense part of the pyramid, is the blocking and tackling section—individual issues or events that must be addressed and often require hand-to-hand combat. For Viacom and CBS in 2004, that was dealing with the firestorm in the wake of the Janet Jackson wardrobe malfunction during the Super Bowl halftime show. For *Newsweek,* it was the desecrated Koran story that the news magazine retracted. At the Pentagon, blocking and tackling issues were a daily—often hourly—occurrence. They ranged from the relatively manageable (say, credit card abuse by Pentagon employees) to intense (say, opposition to our efforts to close outdated installations).

How well one does on those top-tier issues is entirely dependent on the first two levels of the pyramid—the foundation and the advocacy. Disney is a large organization with multiple agendas. But when crises erupt, such as shareholder lawsuits, the reservoir of support it enjoys gives it a decided advantage. The environment in which Disney is considered—whether by policy makers, the media, or consumers—is strong and can withstand and ride out most problems. Disney didn't get to that enviable position overnight. The company's core business commitment to quality entertainment—with a heavy family emphasis—is matched by an intensive communications and government relations effort.

A successful communications program—like a successful battle or business plan—is largely about execution. And the first step in successful execution is rigorous planning. The first most Americans heard of our embedding program in Iraq was when reporters started showing up on their television screens with military units. In truth, intensive planning had been under way for months. Thanks to the tireless efforts of people like Colonel Rhynedance, my deputy Bryan Whitman, and "T" McCreary of the Joint Staff, we took the same approach to the embedding plan that the military would apply to any operation. This book isn't long enough to properly credit all the people—including some thoughtful bureau chiefs and individual correspondents— who worked hard to make embedding work. If success has a thousand fathers, then embedding had a thousand fathers and mothers and aunts and uncles who made it happen.

Starting in the late summer of 2002, we began our own contingency planning as part of the overall plans for a potential war with Iraq. True to military form, we embraced SMEAC as the outline of our plan.

Situation—We were fully aware of a few key fundamentals in late 2002. First of all, public support for a war with Iraq was nowhere near as strong as it had been for going into Afghanistan right after 9/11. Even back then, when the majority of people believed that the Iraqi regime had weapons of mass destruction, many had concerns. People can argue all sides of it, but going into Iraq would be a truly preemptive act. Blessed for more than two centuries with unique geography and good neighbors, most of us had happily embraced the notion that we don't whack somebody unless they whack us first. That's a nice policy in an era in which you can sustain a blow and respond. In the era in which we find ourselves, however—one in which weapons of mass destruction can kill thousands and thousands of people—preemptive action has to be seriously considered and, sometimes, embraced. I was and remain a firm believer in preemptive action in certain circumstances, but I certainly understood the concerns many people had as the nation and the world debated how to deal with Saddam Hussein.

We also knew that a war with Iraq would be about much more than the "kinetic" side of combat. If we went to war, we would be going up against the mother of all liars. Hussein and the Iraqi regime were the absolute best at deception, disinformation, and propaganda. Conservative estimates said that the Iraqis spent a few hundred million dollars every year on these efforts, many of them aimed at the Arab street and global audiences. We needed an effective counterpunch to those substantial efforts, especially during wartime. From past experience, we knew the kinds of things the Iraqi regime would do. We knew they would lie about any military setbacks they suffered and claim all coalition attacks were on innocent civilians. We knew they would dress Iraqi soldiers as civilians to improve their chances at ambushing coalition forces.

We firmly believed that a war with Iraq could be unconventional in many respects. There seemed to be the distinct possibility—back then—that weapons of mass destruction might be used, and that was something neither our forces nor the media had experienced before. We knew that enhanced technologies made it likely that information of all kinds—from straight news reporting to rumors—would travel at lightning speed.

Mission—It was simple: Build and maintain support for the U.S. military and undermine enemy disinformation. Demonstrate the remarkable performance of U.S. forces under difficult circumstances and expose the lies and horrors of the Iraqi regime.

Our mission was simple, and we could explain it. And we did, countless times, as we gained buy-in for the increasingly ambitious plan in the fall and winter of 2002 and 2003.

It was one thing for people like me and "T" and Bryan to advocate the plan. Among us, we had a pretty large reservoir of support and respect throughout the Department of Defense, uniform and civilian. (Okay, "T" and Bryan did; I rode on their coattails.) But we knew real success depended on many factors— most of all, the support of the Pentagon's senior leadership. And it was one thing to presume it. If people think you have the support of the secretary of defense or the chairman of the Joint Chiefs of Staff, it gives you a lot of clout, clout you should use carefully. Given the audacity of the embedding plan, we knew it needed more than a presumption of support from the Rumsfelds and Myerses of the world.

Embedding never would have happened had "T" not thought of the PFOR. Short for "personal for," a PFOR is a message from the chairman of the Joint Chiefs, secretary of defense, or a senior commander. Sent rarely, a PFOR is a clear sign from the sender that he is communicating something of real importance to the subordinate commanders. Chairmen and secretaries seldom send them at all, and we could not find an instance in which a chairman and secretary sent one together. In this case, the PFOR would go to the combatant commanders worldwide and the service chiefs and be copied to enough headquarters to guarantee that just about everybody in a leadership role would receive it. It was "T"'s idea, and it was a brilliant one.

He knew that *our* advocacy would take us only so far. If the chairman and the secretary sent a clear message that communicated embedding's mission and intent, he thought, we would get much better participation from the military. "T"'s joint PA planning team wrote the first draft, and he showed it to me. Editing is always easier than writing, but I had very few changes to suggest, because "T" and the team got it right from the very beginning. The suggestions I did offer up reflected my experience with Rumsfeld's editing. "When in doubt, leave it out. Less is more. Precision, precision, precision."

Once the two of us were happy with the draft, we each watched for the best opening to get our respective bosses' reactions (and, ultimately, signatures). There are never any quiet periods at the Pentagon, and there's no such thing as a good opportunity to raise difficult issues. I decided to run the draft by the secretary in the middle of some other more routine issues as we talked at his stand-up desk. I had briefed him a few times on the embedding program prior to this, so he was generally familiar with where we were headed.

If you know what's good for you, you don't waste Rumsfeld's time. I didn't.

"To really make this work," I started, "we need everyone to know that it has your backing and that of General Myers. It's an extraordinary effort, and I think it deserves something as unusual as a message from you two." I handed him "T"'s draft and held my breath.

The secretary read it quickly—the final message was barely over four hundred words long—and changed next to nothing. The draft made clear the importance of the mission and how imperative it was that all contribute fully to a maximum effort. It was just a draft at this stage, and I needed to reconcile any changes "T" got from the chairman, so we didn't have our first-ever PFOR yet. "T" got a similar response from the chairman. He and the secretary fully expected everyone to embrace the most robust public affairs plan ever conceived for military operations. The message told the military why the mission was important and what was expected of them and assured all that resources would be made available to execute the plan:

> Media coverage of military operations in the coming weeks and months will, to a large extent, shape public perception of the national security environment now and in the years ahead. This holds true for the U.S. public, the public in allied countries, whose opinion can affect the durability of our coalition, and publics in countries where we conduct operations, whose perception of us can affect the cost and duration of our involvement.
>
> Organize for and facilitate access of national and international media to our forces, including those engaged in ground operations. Our goal is to get it right from the start, not days or weeks into the operation. We will commit communications systems and trained joint public affairs teams to facilitate the international press getting a firsthand look at coalition operations as they move forward.
>
> These plans should also support the expeditious movement of media products that tell our story—both good

news and bad—from the front lines. The goal for moving both media products and images should be minutes or hours not days.

Although the PA/Media effort may not be precisely spelled out in the 1003V task list, proceed on the basis that it is an implied task for almost all missions. Our ultimate strategic success in bringing peace and security to this region will come in our long-term commitment to supporting these democratic ideals. Let's tell the factual story—good or bad—before others seed the media with disinformation and distortions as they most certainly will continue to do so. Our people in the field need to tell our story—only Commanders can ensure the media get to the story alongside the troops.

A few days later I took the final draft back to the secretary. At his stand-up desk, as usual, he gave it one more look. "Well," he said, as he took a pen from the top of the desk, "it's a big roll of the dice." And he signed it.

The PFOR had an amazing effect. Everyone from senior brass on down was talking about it when it went out. Sent as a classified document, the PFOR had such an impact that many in the chain of command wanted to distribute and use the message widely, so we got a version of it declassified. Some military public affairs officers took the declassified version into battle with them, believing it bestowed legitimacy on their efforts—it did—and thinking they could pull it out whenever a senior officer objected to their robust efforts to facilitate media coverage.

As I said, many factors and scores of people contributed to embedding's overall success. I am absolutely convinced the one factor that made more difference than anything else, though, was that PFOR. And not every secretary of defense or chairman would have backed such an effort.

When it comes to understanding the information era, Rumsfeld and Myers certainly are ahead of most in public and private life. They're enlightened about the power—both positive and negative—of information and recognize that a willingness to engage on that new front is critical to success. Many wrongly assume the embedding program was a hard sell with people like Rumsfeld and Myers. Nothing could be further from the truth. In many ways, the two of them were ahead of those of us whose main responsibility was communications.

Execution—Execution means different things for different people. For us, it was the strategy that drove the embedding program. And, like all the fundamentals of the embedding program, the strategy was simple: information dominance. Get the good, the bad, and the ugly out in as robust a fashion as possible, primarily through the media. And the plan went beyond just those reporters embedded with forces. We wanted briefings of all sizes and shapes, from Washington, from Qatar (Central Command headquarters in the region), from commanders in the field when technologically possible. Have the news media be the eyes and ears of the war, and give them as many opportunities as possible to execute their jobs.

We employed additional tools to reach people, such as the DefendAmerica Web site, the outreach briefings, e-mail alerts, and others. But especially in the weeks leading up to the start of the war and for a few months after, the news media was the primary means of telling our story.

From March 20 to March 31 alone, there were ten Pentagon press briefings, Rumsfeld appearances on Sunday shows two weeks in a row, and stakeouts on the House and Senate sides of the Capitol after Rumsfeld and Myers briefed Congress. And those numbers don't include individual interviews by senior Pentagon officials, daily briefings in Qatar, and dozens of backgrounders by unit commanders for embedded media.

Administration—Since most people treat communications as an afterthought, few give it the resources and infrastructure it needs. Again, those of us tasked with the information elements of the war were blessed with leaders who realized you can't make this stuff up out of whole cloth. They gave us people, money, equipment, and authority that exceeded what public affairs staff normally get in times of combat.

We exploited their support to the fullest. By applying the same planning and discipline to public affairs that one would use to develop and execute a military operation, we gained more buy-in from the military and were able to achieve much better results. And we could only apply a military mind-set to communications because of people like Rhynedance and Whitman. Intensely focused, they organized this multifaceted, highly sensitive effort with precision and seemingly endless supplies of energy. They made clear who was responsible for what. One person was in charge of the news media with embedded reporters. One handled all of Combat Camera, the in-house still and video photographers who accompanied many of the U.S. forces and supplied footage and photos back to us for briefings, the Web sites, and sometimes the news media.

Others handled the myriad logistical details of sending hundreds of journalists into war with our troops. There were medical issues, liability concerns, diplomatic hurdles, guidance for our PAOs in the field. The level of detailed planning got down to cigarette lighters. As military technical experts met with media counterparts in the months leading up to the war, they learned that some of the vehicles used to transport embedded correspondents didn't have cigarette lighters, a critical issue for those worried about recharging batteries. Working together, the media and the military figured out a way to jerry-rig the vehicles so the reporters and their crews could get the power they needed in the field. The list of tasks went on and on. Given the many parts to the public affairs plan, there was never one book that held the whole plan. But if you had put together all the documents—wire diagrams, lists, talking points, Q&A, charts—that covered every aspect of the plan, the book would have been about five hundred pages long.

What we could and did put in one place was the briefing deck we used for several months as we sought buy-in from the senior Pentagon leadership, as well as our counterparts and their bosses across the river at the White House and State. That deck was about thirty-five pages alone, and I'm not one for long briefing documents. Every page carried important information, though, information that we fine-tuned or changed as we worked through it.

The longest section of that deck was the one entitled "Things That Can Go Wrong." We weren't kidding ourselves about how difficult and risky the embedding could be, and we certainly weren't going to try to convince Rumsfeld and others that there would be anything easy about it. "Things That Can Go Wrong" included: journalists get killed or captured; reporters reveal information that puts a mission or lives at risk (rarely happened); technology fails; commanders deny reporters appropriate access; correspondents can't get their product back. The list went on and on. Sometimes when I was briefing the plan, I thought maybe we overdid it on this section. Looking back, I think it was one of the keys to getting as much buy-in as we did. We were brutally honest with the higher-ups in what the risks were. We didn't pull any punches or gloss over the potential difficulties. But the assumptions we laid out, the planning we demonstrated thanks to the genius and hard work of Rhynedance, Whitman, and company, and the contingency planning we did for those things that would go wrong all helped convince the leadership that the potential benefits outweighed the risks.

Communication—Some people can actually develop meaningful objectives and strategy. A few can actually write the plan that executes the strategy. Where so many people fall down completely is a failure to *communicate* the plan. You know everyone from the CEO to the new employee has to be a communicator. You know that all the sectors of an organization need to be fully integrated in the effort. You know that there will be multiple tools used, depending on the circumstances and the audiences. But you forget to tell people what the plan is. I've seen it happen again and again. Well-meaning people in the public affairs or communications shop of an organization develop a pretty good plan. They might even get a briefing with the CEO. And it ends there for all but the communications staff.

It's somewhat ironic, when you think of it, but I have found that many communications people—either from insecurity or plain stupidity—fail to communicate their own plans to the rest of the organization. That was one mistake we were not going to make in the run-up to the war. Starting in November of 2002 and continuing right up to early March, Rhynedance had me in dozens of Pentagon offices. I briefed the chiefs and vice chiefs of each service. "T" and I briefed Myers and then vice chairman of the Joint Chiefs, General Peter Pace (now chairman). I worked my way through the general counsel, Jim Haynes, and his deputy, Dan Dell'Orto, who had some of the best suggestions, as well as the head of congressional affairs, Powell Moore, and several of his staff. Steve Cambone was director of program analysis and evaluation at the time. Neither he nor his deputy, Rear Admiral Stanley R. Szemborski, escaped the briefing. I spent a few hours with then Lieutenant General Bantz J. (John) Craddock, the secretary's senior military assistant and one of the brightest men in the military. He had terrific suggestions to increase the comfort level of his colleagues in uniform, some of whom were understandably queasy at the thought of keeping company with reporters in the middle of a war.

Getting too far from the building was out of the question, but Rhynedance hooked me up via phone with Lieutenant General Michael "Rifle" DeLong, General Franks's number two at CentCom in Tampa. He, too, made suggestions that increased the likelihood we'd get the buy-in we needed.

After every meeting, Rhynedance, Whitman, "T," and I would hash over the feedback. We'd incorporate some of it, rework the deck, and start briefing again. I wanted the senior leadership to know we valued their insights, needed their help, and counted on their participation if and when the war started. Some people in the building got briefed three or four times, overkill for some of them. One time, a vice chief, unaware that

I was sitting in his outer office waiting to meet with him for the third time in about as many weeks, came out of his office, schedule in hand, and yelled at his assistant, "Please don't tell me Clarke is coming in again on that public affairs plan!"

My third briefing was very short.

I gave Secretary Rumsfeld periodic updates and abbreviated versions of the briefing as 2002 drew to a close. Not until the middle of January did I ask for time to actually sit down in his office and go through the whole plan. There are a few simple tricks to a briefing with Rumsfeld.

1. If you have a briefing deck, number the pages.
2. Don't think you'll impress him with fancy charts and lots of color. As a matter of fact, he has stunning knowledge of the high costs of color versus black-and-white printing and abhors any waste of the taxpayers' money.
3. Be familiar with the material. If you're not, have someone brief it who is. He will have really good questions about the briefing's content. If you don't know the answers, you're toast. And you should be.

Since I had kept him informed along the way, the briefing went pretty easily. And Rumsfeld delivered his highest praise. "Not bad," he said. "Who did it for you?" What a funny guy.

Feeling good about internal support, we turned our focus across the river to counterparts and players in the White House, National Security Council, and the State Department. Clearly we couldn't launch the embedding program without White House support. Dan Bartlett, the White House communications director, was highly supportive of most of our communications efforts and often fought battles on our behalf with other White House staff. Dan, young in years but wise beyond them in judgment, always impressed me with his calm demeanor and considerate style. The White House can be a crushing place to work, and civility is often the first thing to go by the wayside. Not with Dan.

As the embedding program started to take shape, people started to make their concerns known, White House Press Secretary Ari Fleischer among them. And the concerns were important ones. "If this embedding works half as well as you hope," he said in a meeting in Dan's West Wing office, "there's a very real possibility that the American people could see their soldiers hurt or even killed on the battlefield. They might see it on live television. It would be awful!"

I've known Ari since 1988. You can be honest with someone you have known that long in Washington.

"Well, it's the truth, Ari," I responded. "People do get killed in battle. That's the reality, and I think the American people can handle it."

You could sense what was going through the heads of the other communications people in Dan's office that afternoon: "Hmm . . . Ari versus Torie . . . which side do I want to be on?"

Day by day, person by person, we gained the buy-in we needed. But as we briefed up and down the Pentagon's long hallways, we heard one common concern: "Very few of these journalists have any combat or military experience. They could get themselves and others hurt." Bureau chiefs had the same concerns as they began to consider whom they might send with U.S. forces into Iraq. Regular combat could be dangerous enough; in the fall of 2002, *everyone* thought Iraqis' using chemical weapons in a war was a very real possibility. No journalists had encountered that.

I don't know who first developed the idea of military-media boot camps as a way to increase confidence on all sides, although, as with most successes, many take credit for the idea. I do know they exceeded everybody's expectations. Held at four different military bases, the boot camps gave journalists who thought they might be embedded an introductory yet comprehensive look at what they might encounter in battle. For a full week, they'd get briefed on basics like terminology and weapons. They'd learn some first aid and get a taste of what it's like to scramble out of a helicopter in a "hot" landing zone. Those inclined could go through a chamber to experience—briefly—a simulated gas attack. And all were expected to endure the final test—a five-mile hike across hilly terrain with twenty-five-pound packs, with various simulated attacks along the way.

As *U.S. News & World Report* defense correspondent Mark Mazzetti put it in his piece entitled "Dispatches from Media Boot Camp." "The idea behind the boot camps is simple: the more reporters experience military life, the less chance there is that they will slow down, screw up, or report inaccurately about the military unit they are embedded with. It's also a way to make the military brass comfortable with once again letting reporters bum rides on the way to war—a policy that, for the most part, was abandoned after Vietnam."

The Pentagon's general counsel, Jim Haynes, was horrified. He had reservations about the embedding program in general, but—since at that point it was not at all clear we would even go to war—he focused his well-placed angst on the military-media boot camps.

"We cannot do this," he stressed repeatedly at one of Di Rita's morning meetings. He was rightly concerned about our liability if and when journalists were injured. Bad things happen in training exercises as well as combat. Given the assorted sizes, shapes, and conditions of the journalists signing up for the boot camps, it was fairly likely that we'd have at least a few sprained ankles.

"Don't worry," I said. "The service JAGs are covering all the legal bases." As often happened in Di Rita's meeting, someone popped up with some other crisis of the morning and Haynes got distracted. As others talked, I quickly paged Bryan Whitman and George Rhynedance. "Make sure service JAGs cover legal bases for boot camps." Better to beg forgiveness than ask permission.

The morning the first boot camp started, I thought, "Haynes was right." The fifty-eight journalists headed to the first camp were assembled at 0700 at the Pentagon for transport to Quantico. Wearing an odd assortment of Dockers, jeans, state-of-the-art gear from REI, and mostly anxious looks, they seemed more like lost tourists than journalists readying for combat.

How many of these guys might just drop dead of heart attacks? I wondered as I thanked them for participating and watched them head out of the Pentagon parking lot in a drenching rain. The anxiety set in. As the days went by, I checked in frequently with the Marines and with General Andrew Davis, the Marines' chief public affairs officer. "Just don't let anybody die," I kept repeating. "Haynes will kill me."

It turns out we did have a couple of boot camp injuries, but they were mostly of the bumps and scrapes variety. And if it weren't for Rhynedance's quick reaction, I might have suffered the worst injury of all. To show support for the program, Rhynedance and I decided to go to Quantico for the final day and the five-mile hike. I looked forward to getting the reporters' and the Marines' feedback in person. Rhynedance, who spent two hours in the Pentagon for every one I was there, just looked forward to getting out of the building.

We arrived at about eight a.m., just as the reporters were assembling for the hike. By now, the boot camp had become a big news story. Scores of reporters and photographers on assignment crawled all over the place, jockeying for quick interviews with their colleagues who were about to finish up a tough week with a very strenuous hike carrying twenty-five-pound packs. As Rhynedance helped me strap on the pack—I didn't do the helmet, a move I would come to regret—I looked at the reporters. They looked different from a week before. The outfits were even weirder, lots dirtier, and newly decorated. A debate had erupted the evening before as to whether the reporters might be perceived as part of the military—a no-no—rather than bona fide journalists. Masking tape and duct tape that spelled out "PRESS" and "TV" fixed that problem.

But they looked different for another reason. I swear they stood a little taller (that would end about two miles into the hike). They had a strong camaraderie going with their fellow journalists. They clearly were proud of what they had gone through and happy they had made the weeklong commitment.

So we set off—the journalists, their Marine escorts, and about four dozen working media covering every step. It was a beautiful fall day with mist rising. About a forty-minute drive south of Washington, D.C., this part of Quantico seemed hundreds of miles from the Pentagon. Rhynedance and I were having a blast.

It didn't take long for the packs and the hills to take a toll. Faces got red and some reporters quickly fell behind, despite urgings and good-natured taunts from their military escorts. Haynes's face kept flashing before my eyes. One reporter in particular was a concern for me. A veteran journalist, he had seen combat before. But it had been a long time since he'd seen a gym, and it showed.

I slipped back to a Marine PAO. "We have got to make sure he makes it—and makes it alive," I said, gesturing to the reporter, who now looked like he might topple over. It wasn't quite "leave no man behind," but the PAO understood the mission. The next time I looked back, there was the journalist, two Marine escorts on either side, and a Quantico ambulance, following right behind, very slowly, with its flashers on.

Along the route, the Marines executed a series of surprise simulated attacks, of the conventional and unconventional variety. During the week the journalists had put gas masks on in a briefing room and with a Marine's help. Out here, they had to do it rolling on the ground, out of breath, and with a Marine screaming at them to hurry up.

"I am so dead," Fox reporter Bret Baier told us when Rhynedance and I found him under a bush. "This is the third attack, and I haven't gotten my mask on yet." Despite his challenges with the mask—a problem many endured—Bret did better than most of his colleagues and ended the week having earned the healthy respect of several tough Marines.

Rhynedance and I had more fun with every mile. Along the way, we did get feedback from the participants, and it was good. Even the veteran journalists—those who had seen combat—said they were surprised at how useful the week had been. The new ones realized just how challenging combat could be. Similarly, the Marines had a newfound respect for the journalists. "I've got a real appreciation for what they have to do," one young major said to me. "When I jump out of a helicopter in a hot landing zone, I just have to worry about getting to a safe place. These guys," he explained, gesturing to one of the cameramen, "have to get out, think about staying safe, and shoot what's going on." You could feel the confidence building on both sides.

The end of the hike would be a fairly steep hill, but the real challenge would be one more simulated attack, bigger and noisier than all the others. The Marines had tipped us off, so Rhynedance and I jogged ahead to a spot we thought would be out of the line of fire but close enough to see the action. To say we were having fun at others' expense is an understatement. The pack rounded the curve and we could sense the excitement. They picked up the pace a little, knowing, I think, that their fellow journalists were there watching and filming every move.

The explosions started, rivaling in sound and effect a healthy fireworks display at close range. Smoke was everywhere. I was turning to Rhynedance to point something out when he began to hit me on the back of the head—hard—and started yelling at me.

I couldn't hear him and couldn't figure out for the life of me why he kept whacking me in the back of the head. A barrel-chested former gymnast and AH-64 Apache helicopter pilot, Rhynedance could pack a punch. Some of the "simulated" explosions had gone off right near us, landing flaming goo in my hair and melting holes in my Gore-Tex jacket. He kept hitting, and what he was yelling was "Ma'am, your hair's on fire!"

The next thing I knew, *his* jacket was on fire and I was hitting him. Just as we got things under control, the C-SPAN crew covering the day's event came though the smoke to get my reaction to the week's activities.

After checking with Rhynedance to make sure the flames were out, and in between coughs, I gave my endorsement. What I said was "It's all about increasing the comfort level on both sides. It is to everybody's advantage for there to be as much media access to the military as possible. Obviously, there are safety concerns and considerations. There are concerns that you want an operation to be successful. The more we know about each other's business, the better we can do it."

What I was thinking was "My burnt hair smells really bad, and Haynes is going to kill me if he finds out."

For the next few days back in the building, I made sure Haynes never walked or sat behind me. I was afraid he would ask why a big chunk of my hair was missing.

Burnt hair notwithstanding, the boot camps did go far to increase the comfort level on both sides. Bureau chiefs and flag officers alike began to realize that most people were taking matters very seriously and investing significant time and effort into what could be the most unconventional war fought in a long time. Over 750 journalists—domestic and foreign—requested slots in the boot camps. Several bureau chiefs told me they thought that even if there weren't a war, the boot camps had been a valuable exercise and should be continued in some fashion.

Meanwhile, our commitment to transparency extended to the embedding plan itself. As Whitman and his team worked through the myriad details of how actual embedded reporters would interact with their units, he included news organizations in his planning. Rather than guessing (although Bryan's guesses, based on a lot of experience, were pretty good) at how public affairs guidance for the field might work, he shared drafts with news organization heads, bureau chiefs, and correspondents to get their reaction. They made some good suggestions, most of which we could live with. Just as important, Bryan's inclusion of them in our planning process was yet another sign of our serious intent to find ways to facilitate media coverage of what could be a very unconventional war.

The very act of inclusion was a way of communicating the plan. And by being inclusive, whether with our colleagues in the building or in the White House or with the news media, we increased awareness, participation, and, ultimately, our chances for success.

Such a scientific approach to communications is still more the exception than the rule. But as public and private sector leaders begin to realize the enormous impacts on their bottom lines of the information era, they will be forced to embrace truly twenty-first-century communications. And that includes lots of discipline, organization, and good old-fashioned work.

CHAPTER 7

What Was I Thinking?

———

Speak up, shut up, or
get out of the way.

———

As much as I advocate engaging in a story and making sure your side gets out, sometimes it's best just to say nothing and know when to stand down—or just get others to shut up.

Colonel Rhynedance was fastidious about most things. He was especially obsessive-compulsive—in a good way—about phone messages. Given the daily volume of incoming calls, though, there was no way I could return all of them, and sometimes it wasn't appropriate for me to do so. A call on the details of the anthrax vaccine program, for instance, could be much better handled by Jim Turner, our resident expert on health care.

Rhynedance knew how to triage the calls and how to field and traffic them. He also knew when he should tell me about a call even if I wasn't going to be the one to return it. In the early weeks of the Iraq war, the incoming was immense. One day, returning from a meeting in Rumsfeld's office, I ticked off a few follow-up action items and then went through the messages with Rhynedance.

In the middle of the pile—most of them from Pentagon correspondents, bureau chiefs, and the like—there was one that prompted Rhynedance to say, "Oh, you're going to love this one, ma'am." It was a message from Robin Givhan of the *Washington Post*. Unbeknownst to either of us, she covered fashion for the *Post*. Evidently, she had noticed that I often wore bright colors and wanted to talk with me about my clothing choices.

"Not a chance," I said to Rhynedance, asking him to call her back himself and politely decline the opportunity to discuss my clothes. It crossed my mind briefly that in the first few weeks of the war one might think the paper had more important things to cover. But that was the last I thought of it.

Several days later, I headed up to the 0600 operations meeting with Rumsfeld, Myers, and other senior military and civilian staff. Tightly organized and focused, this was the most important meeting of the day and—not surprising, given the timing—a serious event that one did not want to miss.

Just to be on the safe side—and to get another cup of coffee before the meeting got rolling—I always tried to arrive a few minutes early. As people shuffled for caffeine and seats, the SecDef came in and headed over to the coffee wearing a bright red fleece vest and a rich purple and red tie. It looked pretty sharp.

"Very spiffy attire today, sir," I said as I moved to let him get at the coffee. Without looking up as he poured, the SecDef said quietly, "I wore it for *you*." I had no idea what he meant, so I asked him.

"Well, given the Style section story today, Joyce thought I should wear this in solidarity." I hadn't read the Style section since early 2001, so I repeated myself. "I have *no* idea what you're talking about."

"Oh," he said, now looking up at me with a mischievous smile, before returning to his seat and starting the meeting. "Then you'd better take a look at the paper." I made the silly assumption that the meeting was important, so I didn't worry much about his comments. After all, I thought, how bad could something in the Style section be? I should have known better.

As the meeting broke up and we all headed for the hallways, the SecDef called after me, "You'd better take a look, Torie."

I called Rhynedance on the way back. "What's up with the Style section?" I asked. Rhynedance read the Style section less frequently than I did. He said he'd find it as I headed back. He was never one to hold back bad news; Rhynedance's face said it all when I walked into the office.

"Oh, it's bad," he said. "It" was a huge Style section piece that covered—in great detail—my choice of clothing. It included heavy criticism for what some people saw as inappropriate attire, given the seriousness of my surroundings and responsibilities. The piece was too darn long to read—not that I had the stomach or the time for it anyway. But you couldn't miss the pictures—seemingly dozens of them—filling an inside page. The jacket that drew the most ridicule was a Louis Féraud that can only be described as asymmetrical patchwork. Some called it the "Partridge Family Bus" jacket; others thought it looked like a Mondrian with buttons. What can I say? It was in my closet, so I wore it.

I sure didn't have time to worry about the article at the time. And I certainly didn't expect what happened. All at once, our office got a flood of calls and e-mails from people whose emotions ranged from aggravation to outrage that the *Post* had focused on something as trivial as my clothes at a time of war. They were young and old, male and female. They were average citizens and senior correspondents from across Washington and the country. One of the best reporters in Washington said she was going to call Donny Graham, the publisher of the *Post*, and "tell him just how despicable this is." A *Post* reporter e-mailed me with "I thought we had covered every aspect of this war. I was SOOOOOO wrong!"

I was stunned by the volume of responses—and touched that Secretary and Mrs. Rumsfeld displayed both thoughtfulness and a sense of humor. Lots of people wanted me—or others on my behalf—to respond in some fashion. My husband, God bless him, had a scathing letter ready to go—his own version of Harry Truman's threat to punch out a critic who had given his daughter's public singing debut a rotten review.

Rhynedance and I did a couple of gut checks during the day and remained convinced—despite the temptation—that the best and obvious choice was not to engage. One reporter actually hunted down my mother in Sewickley, Pennsylvania, to get her reaction to the "scandal," as he called it. It never occurred to me that the story might be a big deal, so I hadn't given her or my dad a heads-up. Of course, I didn't call them on 9/11 either, so maybe my judgment on these things is flawed. Anyhow, the reporter filled in my mother—feeding her some of the choice quotes—and asked for her reaction.

"Well," she said, demonstrating that common sense and quick thinking are the best communication skills out there, "if that's the meanest thing they ever say about Torie, I think she'll be okay." I was. The next day I wore purple.

My mother has impressive communication skills, so whatever strengths I have in that department may well come from her. Early on, I learned from her the power of words.

Being the youngest of five girls growing up in suburban Pittsburgh can be challenging under any circumstances. For me, the problems were compounded by the fact that my older sisters were everything I was not. They were beautiful, very smart, athletically gifted, and exceptional students. The three oldest ones could sing Gilbert and Sullivan a cappella, for God's sake.

As my sisters excelled their way through St. James, our school, and the local tennis club, they got used to being number one in their classes, first on their teams, and admired by just about everyone who met them. I got used to hearing the same question over and over. "Are you going to be as smart and talented as your older sisters?" family friends and relatives would ask. I never had an answer, but I had a gnawing sense of dread as I approached school age. This does not sound good, I'd think to myself.

One colleague of my father's, Dr. John Yukovich, was the worst. I am sure he meant no harm, but his entire conversational repertoire seemed to consist of "Are you going to be as smart and talented as your sisters?" This to a five-year-old. Tall, thin, and often wearing black, he would pat my head every time he saw me and ask the question. I didn't know then what the grim reaper was, but I felt like I was meeting my maker every time.

My mother knew it too and was fed up with Yukovich. As she and I walked toward the grocery store one day, he was coming out. There was no escape. "He's going to ask me again," I cried, clutching my mother's hand. "I just know it. He's going to ask me again."

My mother stopped and bent down to put her face close to mine. "When he asks you, just say, 'No, but you can't blame me because I am illegitimate.'" At five, I had no idea what illegitimate meant, but I did know how to take direction. And I trusted my mother completely. Dr. Yukovich asked his question, and I delivered my line flawlessly.

His mouth opened and closed a couple of times, but he couldn't say a word. And he never asked me the question again.

In cards, you can't beat something with nothing. In communications, sometimes nothing is the very best you can achieve.

- Know the difference between an issue in which you *should* be engaged and one in which there is no return on investment.
- If you have a surefire one-liner that will stop someone in his tracks, like those my mother employed, use it.
- If not, keep your mouth shut. Maybe, just maybe, the offending issue will have a slightly shorter shelf life.

If it seems like I've spent a long time dwelling on how to deal with bad stories and mistakes, it's because I enjoy sharing war stories about missteps, and heaven knows I've made plenty.

Probably I've made more than my share. But I'm pretty sure of this too: so do most people in visible positions. It's just part of life. And if you're in a public position—whether you're a CEO or a Pentagon spokesperson—I'd offer this rule of thumb: if you aren't admitting mistakes at least six times a year, you aren't being honest. Seriously.

So in that vein, allow me to leave this topic with one last reminiscence about a total, top-to-bottom screwup. If you take nothing else from this chapter, please remember what I'm about to tell you. If you're ever assistant secretary of defense for public affairs, *do not* take your children to a press briefing.

Dierks Bentley's song "What Was I Thinking" often comes to mind when I think about one day in March 2003. Major combat operations were under way in Iraq, and many people were working around the clock. Despite the torrent of coverage and interest in the war, we had most things under control at the Pentagon from a communications standpoint. So, of course, when you have one area of your life clicking, something has to break. And that's when the perfect storm occurred on my home front.

My husband, Brian, who seldom traveled, was out of town. Brian significantly changed his life and schedule so I could do my job at the Pentagon. He had managed more than one crisis for the family. There was the time, just a few weeks after 9/11, when our house was broken into in broad daylight. Brian handled it all—the police, the locksmith, everything. Early the next morning, Rumsfeld informed me that we would have to leave for the Middle East that afternoon. Around lunchtime, Brian called me on his cell phone and informed me that he was sitting in his car in front of the house. I could hear sirens in the background.

"You want the good news or the bad news?" he asked.

"The good news."

"There is none," he replied. "The robbers came back and stole the van."

"Wow, that stinks," I said, before delivering the capper: "By the way, I have to go to the Middle East this afternoon."

The next year, while the planning for a potential war in Iraq was reaching full pitch, Brian was at the playground with the kids. Devan, our daughter, was handling the controls—or at least had her hands on the controls—of a toy bulldozer, the kind with a shovel on the end, when she wheeled it around and smacked her younger brother Charlie right in the head. I don't think it was on purpose. A gusher of blood ensued, naturally, which sent all three kids into a frenzy of screaming. Brian ditched the kids' bikes at the park and hoofed it back to the house to get the car. That night, I came home to find Charlie's blood-saturated shirt soaking in the sink and Brian asleep on the couch next to an empty bottle of wine.

So, needless to say, there was no complaining on the rare occasion he left town for a day or two. Our amazing babysitter, Monica, was sick. She called late at night to let me know she thought she was okay, that she might be able to make it in by late morning. I had to ask a few questions to figure out she was in the emergency room and it was highly unlikely that she would be out anytime soon. Monica seldom got sick and could always be counted on. And the kids didn't have school that day. The perfect storm.

Being the multitasker I am, and feeling good with how things were going at the Pentagon, I thought, No problem. I can handle this. I'll take the kids to work.

You're probably already asking yourself what I was thinking. Actually, just taking them to the building was no big deal. They were there a lot, visiting on weekends, conning my colleagues out of candy, and, usually, behaving themselves.

What made this day different was the timing. General Stan McChrystal and I were scheduled to hold a press briefing that day around lunchtime. The usual cast of dozens was packed in my office around the conference table prepping. Colin, Devan, and Charlie, ages eight, six, and four, respectively, were on the floor in a corner, happily eating cheeseburgers and french fries from the mess. The usual routine for them, if they happened to be in the building during a briefing, was for them to watch it in my office. This day quickly became anything but usual.

Maybe it was seeing McChrystal in person; he's very impressive-looking. Maybe it was boredom at hanging out in my office. Whatever the reason, Colin and his sidekicks announced that they wanted to watch the briefing live in the briefing room.

"Absolutely not," I shot back, all the right instincts kicking in. All briefings were important. We were in the early weeks of the war, and there was a lot to focus on without worrying about my kids. The kids were crushed but didn't argue, so I thought that issue was over. And that's when McChrystal—on whom I place much of the blame for this whole affair—took their side.

"Oh, come on," he said, with a remarkably pleading look on his face for a Special Ops guy. "Don't be so mean. Look at them. They'll be good."

And then all his guys—and they were all guys—chimed in.

"Yeah, come on," they whined on behalf of my kids. "They'll be good. Don't be mean."

My kids couldn't believe their luck: lots of big guys in uniform taking their side against their mother. It doesn't get any better. That's when I made the first mistake of the morning. Looking at the hopeful faces—on the uniformed guys and my kids—I said, "OK, on one condition. You three sit in the back and do not say a word!"

All the heads nodded up and down in agreement, and Colin started high-fiving some of his new comrades in arms. They were happy; I was concerned.

So the kids headed into the briefing room, and McChrystal and I tied up a few loose ends before we walked in. Given the timing, the briefings were packed, and this one was no exception. The seats were filled with over a hundred correspondents. There were TV news cameras jammed on the riser in the back of the room, and to stage right of the podium, the cutaway cameras. Still photographers filled all the nooks and crannies on either side of the room.

As McChrystal and I walked in, I could see—through the eyes in the back of my head—that the kids were sitting in chairs as instructed. So far, so good.

We started the briefing—as we always did—with some prepared remarks and then launched into the questions. There were a ton of them, reporters were raising their hands in droves, and the exchange was lively and rapid-fire. McChrystal and I worked the first few rows of reporters, and I glanced to the back of the room. And something in me twitched when I saw my kids, still sitting quietly in their chairs. Only a mother would notice something like this, but—while I answered some question about the Third Infantry Division hauling up to Baghdad—I realized that my kids were sitting up very straight in their chairs. They never sit up straight, which is a constant source of nagging on my part. Something was up, but I had to focus on the questions.

Still answering questions, I glanced to the back of the room, and that's when I started to wonder what I'd been thinking earlier. A lightbulb had gone on over Colin's head. He had finally figured it out, and I could tell what was going through his head as he watched the interaction in the room.

She meant don't say a word unless you raise your hand first! he thought to himself. And then he raised his hand.

I stifled a laugh and then started to panic. It was an unwritten rule of mine never to laugh publicly at the Pentagon. My old—and well-deserved—reputation for being a smart-ass had no place there, and good friends like Margaret Tutwiler admonished me early and often to keep that side of my personality under wraps.

Some people said I executed that policy to a fault and could have lightened up some on the job. I would privately, but I couldn't at that podium. We dealt with life-and-death issues every day. The people for whom I worked—the men and women in uniform, risking their lives on a daily basis—deserved the utmost in decorum and responsibility from people like me. Until this day, I had done pretty well.

Maybe it was Colin's skinny arm sticking in the air and the hopeful look on his face. Maybe it was the confused looks on Devan's and Charlie's faces as they watched their older brother. Whatever it was—as McChrystal and I continued to address myriad issues—I realized that I was about to start laughing. My face got red, and I could feel sweat start to go down my back.

Still answering questions, I looked over again. (I know, you're thinking about that Dierks Bentley song again.) Devan

211

and Charlie were not about to be left out. They too had raised their hands and were looking every bit as determined as some of the veteran correspondents in the room.

By that point, I knew I was going to lose it, and McChrystal wasn't far behind. If you're at that podium, you can lean back a little bit and mumble a few words to the person next to you without much fear that the mikes will pick it up.

"Not good" is all I could hear from McChrystal, and he wasn't talking about the questions from the Pentagon press corps. You have to know McChrystal to appreciate what it takes to rattle him. An Army brigadier general and vice director of operations for the Joint Chiefs when I first met him, McChrystal is now a two-star and head of the Joint Special Operations Command out of Fort Bragg. An Army Ranger, McChrystal rose fast to the top of the military's elite Special Operations Forces (SOF). He embraces the SOF mantra of "quiet professional" and probably would have done anything rather than be the regular briefer for the Joint Staff. But he did it and did it very well. Until my kids showed up.

Now I was in full panic, and the reporters in the front rows had started to catch on. If they see you looking somewhere, they look. Glancing to the back of the room, they saw three little arms in the air, fingers hopefully wiggling. The reporters started laughing, and CNN's Barbara Starr made things worse. Sitting in the front row, she started lobbying, quietly, on the kids' behalf.

"Come on, let them ask a question," she said under her breath while looking innocently down at her notebook.

That's it, I think to myself. I have to get them out of my line of sight or I will break up completely. So I turned. And I turned a lot, hoping my peripheral vision wouldn't be good enough to see them. I was practically perpendicular to McChrystal and facing the cutaway cameras to the right. Normally, in a briefing, the cutaways would be focused on the podium. Not this time. All of them were shooting something at the back of the room.

Oh no, is all I could think as I wheeled around in dread.

Colin, Devan, and Charlie decided I wasn't calling on them because I couldn't see them, so they stood on their chairs and started flailing their arms wildly. Since he was the smallest guy in the room, Charlie was jumping up as high as he could.

That was it. Now I was laughing, McChrystal was laughing, and most of the press in the room were cracking up. I tried to end the briefing by turning to Jim Miklaszewski of NBC. "Last question, Mik," I blurted to him in the front row. Mik was laughing so hard at this point, he just waved me away. Colin couldn't stand it any longer.

"That is *so* unfair, Mom!" he screamed from the back of the room, loud enough for everyone to hear.

So the communications lesson is an easy one. Think twice— no, think three or four times—before you take small children to a press briefing.

CHAPTER 8

It's About One Thing

---

*The age of transparency
has begun.*

The thing I will always remember first is the spectacular crystal blue brilliance of the day. Not a trace of typical Washington, D.C., late-summer haze hung in the air. At five thirty or six a.m., my daily commute was early enough to avoid Washington's brutal downtown rush-hour traffic. As I cut across the bridge spanning the Potomac and parked on the concourse outside the Pentagon's eastern edge, the sky—completely clear and utterly cloudless—seemed to stretch on forever.

Arriving in my office in the Pentagon's outer ring, I thumbed through the previous day's news clippings and reviewed the day's schedule with my staff. Among the many challenges of being assistant secretary of defense for public affairs, an ornate title that refers to the person who runs the communications shop, or tries to, is that you have to get in before dawn to have any prayer of getting ahead of the game—a prayer that is, on even the calmest of days, rarely answered.

At seven thirty, I headed one flight of stairs up and a short jog down the hall to Secretary Rumsfeld's suite of offices, where around five or six senior staffers huddled with Larry Di Rita— Rumsfeld's right-hand man—for our daily meeting. The main topic of discussion was a major address Rumsfeld had delivered the day before on his ambitious and highly controversial plan to reorganize and transform the Pentagon bureaucracy. Since my arrival on the job a few months earlier, we had fought—mostly unsuccessfully—to gain traction on the issue. It was a classic illustration of the dilemma of communicating change: the organized cadres of people who are threatened tend to pay a lot more attention than the public at large who stand to benefit. Unless we could get the American people to care, we would be swamped by the deeply entrenched interests whose places at the ample Pentagon trough were in jeopardy. Rumsfeld's speech was on the front pages of several newspapers around the country. Finally, it seemed, we were making progress.

Around eight, I headed back downstairs for the public affairs team's morning meeting in my office, followed by a short session to discuss the issues journalists would be asking about later that day in a regularly scheduled briefing. The big one was Operation Amber Fox, a weapons-collection program in Macedonia. Amber Fox wasn't going well.

Noting the military's often peculiar way of naming things, I said, "I know I'm not the military expert in the room, but maybe if we had called it something like Operation Weapons Collection, we'd have gotten more weapons turned in." We'd been discussing it for days, and every time I heard the name of the operation, I laughed. "I know that name somehow," I kept saying. "This is driving me crazy." Finally, a Google search revealed the answer. "Hey, guys," I announced proudly. "Amber Fox is a porn star."

The discussion went on for another minute or two. Admiral Craig Quigley, sitting to my right, looked at the bank of televisions behind me. "It doesn't matter what you say about Macedonia," he said, pointing to the screens. "Because this is now the story of the day."

Three televisions along the top row were showing distant shots of two skyscrapers. A large hole had been blown into the side of one tower. Black smoke was pouring out. The cable anchors were stammering. *Something has hit the World Trade Center,* they said. *We think it's a small plane.*

It was September 11, 2001.

Brigadier General John W. Rosa, then the deputy director for operations on the Joint Staff (now a retired lieutenant general and president of The Citadel) and a veteran Air Force pilot, told me later that many real aviators knew it was a deliberate hit the instant they heard about the first crash. The sky was just too clear: it wasn't possible for an experienced pilot to hit anything by mistake that day.

At first, though, it didn't look like a ton of damage—not to the rest of us. The sheer enormity of the World Trade Center defied any comprehension of its scale. From a distance, the small-plane theory—perhaps a traffic plane got too close and grazed the tower—seemed plausible. Still, the people in the plane must have been killed, and there surely were casualties in the building too. Those poor people, I kept thinking. Those poor people.

I dialed Di Rita.

"You watching this?" I asked.

"Yeah."

"Has anyone told the secretary?" Even in the accidental crash scenario, the military might be involved in some way. Rumsfeld needed to know.

"We sent a note in to him," Di Rita replied. Rumsfeld was in the middle of a breakfast meeting with several members of Congress. The administration had asked for an increase in the defense budget, and Congress was skittish. Someday, Rumsfeld told the members that morning, there will be an event—I don't know when, I don't know how, but it'll be bad—and you won't want to have been on the wrong side of this issue.

Di Rita and I were watching our TVs as we spoke. Suddenly, at near-blinding speed, a large black silhouette—the shape seemed vaguely like an airplane—slammed into the side of the second tower. I blurted out the first thing that came to my mind.

"Holy shit."

After giving a few instructions to the staff, I shot back up to Rumsfeld's office, making notes in a black binder along the way of initial steps we needed to take—establishing contact with the president, the vice president, CIA Director George Tenet, Secretary of State Colin Powell, the Federal Aviation Administration—and what the Pentagon would be saying about it.

Di Rita and I pushed through Rumsfeld's door. Secretaries

of defense traditionally use Blackjack Pershing's old desk. Rumsfeld uses the desk top for files but prefers to stand behind a lectern-shaped desk instead, which was where Di Rita and I found him, reviewing his schedule to see what appointments he could cancel.

"Sir," Di Rita said, "I think your *entire* schedule is going to be different today."

By that point, just minutes after the second plane had hit and confirmed for everyone that the United States was under a massive and coordinated terrorist attack, the Pentagon's Executive Support Center (ESC)—the place where the building's top leadership goes to coordinate military operations during national emergencies—was spinning up into operation. Cables, the Pentagon's state-of-the-art communications hub, was busily establishing secure two-way video hookups with the White House and other key agencies. Rumsfeld told Di Rita and me to get down there and wait for him. In the meantime, he would get his daily intelligence briefing, which was already scheduled for nine thirty.

Di Rita and I headed down the long hallway toward the ESC. We were buzzed in through the heavy meat-locker door. Inside one conference room, multiple screens showed live television images of the World Trade Center. That's the post–Cold War world for you, I thought: here we were in the Pentagon's war room, with instant access to satellite images and intelligence sources peering into every corner of the globe, and we were watching the cable networks to get the latest information. The towers were still standing, but it was clear a full-scale humanitarian catastrophe was under way.

Steve Cambone, another top Rumsfeld aide, was there. Cambone possesses two highly useful qualities for a leader in the defense establishment: blazing brilliance and near-pathological pessimism. We used to call him Eeyore. Within moments of the second plane's hitting, Cambone knew it was a terrorist attack and had deduced that al Qaeda was probably behind it. No other group was sophisticated enough to pull it off.

At that point, the only thing we knew for sure was that terrorists were hijacking planes and using them as massive suicide bombs. The top priority had to be getting every plane in the air back on the ground. We were discussing how when we felt a jarring thump and heard a loud but still muffled explosion. The building seemed to have shifted.

"Wow," I said. "It must have been a car bomb."

"A bomb of some kind," Di Rita replied.

One staffer, who frequently used the center for meetings, pointed to the ceiling.

"No, it's just the heating and cooling system. It makes that noise all the time."

The notion of a jetliner attacking the Pentagon was exactly that unfathomable back then. Our eyes were glued to television screens showing two hijacked planes destroying the World Trade Center and it still didn't occur to any of us, certainly not me, that one might have just hit our own building.

For the second time in under an hour I said, "I know I'm not the military expert in the room," and hazarded a guess that what we had just heard was not the heating and cooling system.

The ensuing minutes after American Airlines Flight 77 hit the Pentagon's west wall were a blur of activity. We scrambled for information about what exactly *had* happened, how many were hurt or killed, and analyzed what we could do to prevent further attacks. It wasn't even ten a.m. yet. Someone looked up and asked where Rumsfeld was.

"He's out of the building," another person answered. I was relieved. The country was under attack: security measures for those in the line of presidential succession had kicked in. Rumsfeld must have been rushed away to a secure location off-campus.

Around ten fifteen, Rumsfeld walked into the command center, his suit jacket over his shoulder and his face and clothes smeared with ashes, dirt, and sweat. He smelled like smoke—not acrid smoke, especially, more like he had spent hours sitting around a campfire. He was quiet, deadly serious, completely cool.

"I'm quite sure it was a plane and I'm pretty sure it's a large plane," he said. A former naval aviator, Rumsfeld knew the smell of jet fuel. For those of us in the command center, it was the first real—and horrible—confirmation that a plane had hit the building.

Rumsfeld had been in the middle of his intelligence briefing when the plane hit. From his office, it was clear it was more than a car bomb—and certainly not the air conditioning. Rumsfeld took off running down the hall to find out what was going on, one man from his security detail chasing him down. A thousand feet from his office, the smoke was too thick to proceed. Darting down a flight of stairs, Rumsfeld headed out of the building, ran around to the crash site, and started helping emergency workers load victims onto stretchers. When someone had said the secretary was "out of the building," he meant it literally: he was *outside* the building.

Rumsfeld was our first eyewitness. The explosion was enormous. Chunks of what appeared to be an airplane were spread out over a huge expanse. It was inconceivable that anyone in the plane, if that's what it was, could have survived, and the damage to the building itself was devastating.

Rumsfeld pulled out a yellow legal pad, took his seat at the head of a conference table, and wrote down three categories by which his thinking would be organized the rest of the day: what we needed to do immediately, what would have to be under way quickly, and what the military response would be. The most immediate priority was preventing further attacks. There were already reports of a plane down in Pennsylvania. A handful of commercial airliners didn't immediately respond to our orders to stay clear of American airspace, and similar problems might arise. We had to assume other planes had been or would be hijacked. An ominous issue—whether American fighter pilots would have to shoot down civilian airliners—loomed.

I was taking notes and feeding what information I could to my team outside. Some cell phones worked, some didn't. Within an hour of the attack, we began responding to the thousands of media inquiries with what information we had—which wasn't much. My instructions to our team were direct: they were to say *nothing* of which we weren't absolutely sure. At the same time, I was convinced we had to get as much information out as possible. As soon as the plane hit the Pentagon, Washington would be in pandemonium—a metro area of more than 4 million people justifiably believing they were under attack. The best antidote to panic was information—not more than we had, certainly not speculation, but as much as possible.

Quarters in the command center were cramped. The area— a rabbit's nest of cubicles surrounding the main conference room—was packed with senior military and civilian leaders, not to mention being ringed with at least a dozen technicians from Cables. Smoke from the explosion was already permeating the building. At one point, it got so thick that we had to move to another facility—a similarly equipped room used by the Joint Chiefs of Staff—in search of some better air.

Military and civilian officials alike were concerned about the conditions in the command center as well as the possibility of another attack. They periodically urged Rumsfeld to get out of the building. Rumsfeld ordered aides to make contingency plans in case the lack of breathable air—by this time, everyone was intermittently coughing and choking even within the well-sealed confines of the command center—made it necessary. Rumsfeld just ignored those urging him to leave the building.

About forty-five minutes after the Pentagon attack, I ducked into a hallway, grabbed one of the few open phone lines, and punched in my husband's office number. Our three kids—then ages six, four, and three—were at school. I wanted Brian to pick them up and get them home. It hadn't occurred to me that I might be in any personal danger. By that point the Pentagon was probably the safest, most heavily guarded building in America. But I was concerned about the kids.

Brian's assistant, a terrific woman named Mary Lou, picked up the phone on the first ring, heard my voice, and didn't bother with small talk. "He's in the car on his way to get the kids right now."

I dialed Brian's car phone.

"The streets are jammed out here," he said. "People don't know what to do."

That confirmed what my gut was telling me. I went back and

got Rumsfeld's attention. We had to communicate that the Pentagon was up and running and that the government wasn't in chaos. That was the most important reassurance we could provide, and I also wanted those SOBs to know they'd failed. Rumsfeld agreed. For the rest of the day—and the days to come—that one message would dominate every message we put out: "The Pentagon is up and running."

During his next conversation with Cheney, Rumsfeld raised the need for a clear, confidence-instilling message. As he spoke, I shoved handwritten points in front of him. "Statement for VP to make—doing everything appropriate to prevent further attacks—grounded all commercial aircraft and ordered military to shoot down threats—all facilities at highest level of alert—very important that people remain calm and stay off the streets. Emergency vehicles must be able to get through. Here's the point: we're taking care of our *own*—federal employees. We have *not told* others—real people—what to do? Stay home? Go to a basement? What?"

Cheney agreed that a firm statement of confidence was in order. The president would make one as soon as Air Force One landed at Barksdale Air Force Base in Louisiana, where it had been diverted as a security precaution. As for what the public should do, we just didn't know. We watched the statement in the command center. It was brief and tough.

"Make no mistake," Bush said. "The United States will hunt down and punish those responsible for these cowardly acts."

General Hugh Shelton, the chairman of the Joint Chiefs of Staff, was rushing back from an overseas trip. In the meantime, General Richard Myers, then the vice chairman and Rumsfeld's nominee to replace Shelton, was the senior uniformed military official. He and Rumsfeld were never more than a few inches from each other. At twelve forty-five Myers reported that a Korean Airlines flight was inbound from Asia squawking the hijack code, a covert signal to air traffic controllers that the plane had been commandeered. It was over Alaska and headed east.

"I want to tie up the rules of engagement," Rumsfeld said, asking again about the orders for pilots who might have to shoot down hijacked planes. "We need granularity here. This is not simple for a pilot, especially if he knows he's shooting down a plane over a civilian area like Washington." I began to think through the plans for how we would announce such an extraordinary act, if it had to occur.

Soon we got word that the Korean plane was sending the hijack code by mistake. The other stray airliners were located and grounded. The rules of engagement were ironed out, but, fortunately, never had to be employed.

Rumsfeld turned to Myers and raised the issue of our military response to the attacks.

"We're going to need to think big," Rumsfeld said.

"You bet," Myers replied. Even before he took office, Rumsfeld was concerned that the United States had developed a reputation as a nation that could be picked at and attacked without repercussions. Our talk was more aggressive than our actions. Rumsfeld's concern was less the actual scope of our response than that we follow through on our words. He mentioned this in his first conversation with Bush before his appointment as secretary of defense, and he revisited the issue now with Myers.

Rumsfeld had a firm hand on the tiller in the command center. But the building itself, of course, *was* in a certain amount of chaos, including the hall that housed the public affairs team and the press. Alarms were still ringing at top volume two hours after the plane hit the building. Journalists were evacuated with everyone else, nearly twenty-five thousand people.

As soon as the evacuation began, our public affairs staff started making arrangements for an off-site press center. Bryan Whitman and Admiral Quigley raced a quarter mile toward the highway to a Navy exchange gas station run by CITGO. After a quick talk with the management—to whom we later presented a DOD commendation for their help—they commandeered the place for the press.

When my calls would get through to Whitman and Quigley, they would share with the media gathered around gas pumps what I told them. As the day wore on, it became clear we should get someone on camera who had stayed in the building and could testify that it was still working and that leadership was in place. We tracked down Chief John Jester, who ran security for the Pentagon and had stayed in the building after the attack. He could address for the media the physical status of the building and security measures under way. I could speak to the attack itself and try to tamp down some of the wild speculation already flying. He and I got in a car and headed over to the CITGO to brief the media. As we pulled away, I saw the crash site for the first time. The devastation was unimaginable. I felt I was looking out the window at a Hollywood action flick. An entire side of not just any heavily fortified building was blown to pieces. As we approached the CITGO, I saw dozens upon dozens of reporters. Satellite trucks were lined up all down the side of the road.

Jester and I stepped inside the gas station. The refrigerators were completely cleared: the media bought anything left after most of the ice and drinks were carried down to the first responders at the crash site. After a brief conversation with Whitman, Quigley, and the other staff on site, Jester and I walked into the middle of the throng of journalists. My statement was brief. It was a terrible day for the country. Our thoughts and prayers were with the wounded and their loved ones. The secretary of defense was in the building directing our effort, and he was in constant communication with the president, the vice president, the Joint Staff, and the National Security Council.

The press nailed us with a barrage of questions. How many were dead? Had we confirmed that all the top brass were alive? Time and again I replied that we did not know and would not speculate. It was the only truthful answer. The reporters grew agitated. As I looked out on the crowd, I saw their faces. They were rattled. They too had been in a building under attack, and they were standing under an open sky that might turn deadly again at any minute.

As Jester and I pulled away in the security car to head back to the building, I looked back. Sitting on an island below the gas pumps was a reporter, one of the best and most seasoned network correspondents, with his head in his hands and his notebook on the ground.

When I got back to the command center, the news was good and bad. Some of the planes not responding initially to instructions to avoid U.S. airspace had diverted; a few were still causing concern. The smoke was still thick.

Rumsfeld looked up and saw the dozens of people working there. He turned to Myers. "We ought to tell these people they can leave and be with their families."

"Sir," Myers answered, "they're not going to leave unless you do. They'll all go down with you."

Throughout the day, I had tried to scribble down some notes of the conversations and actions in the command center. They were sketchy at best, but I thought they might help in any after-action reports that certainly would be done. As I took down Myers's words, it was the first time it occurred to me that the Pentagon was still in jeopardy. I jotted a notation that was part nervous reaction and part gallows' humor: "Uh-oh."

Rumsfeld took a call from Senators Carl Levin and John Warner, the chairman and ranking member of the Senate Armed Services Committee. Rumsfeld had their wholehearted support, they promised. They were there for whatever he needed. Rumsfeld suggested they come over to the building. When they arrived, the three called the president.

"We will find these people and they will suffer the consequences," Bush said. "Everybody needs to be focused on that objective."

"Our enemy is clear," Levin replied. "We're going to focus on what unites us. We're very firm, very resolute. We'll be totally arm-in-arm and look forward to joining your leadership." Warner updated Bush on the activities in the Pentagon. "They're working full-time right now. We're standing foursquare with you."

By now it was late afternoon, and Rumsfeld, Levin, and Warner and a small handful of aides went out to the crash site. All of us had seen distant camera shots of the devastation on television throughout the day, but to see it up close was stunning. Thousands of metal shards covered everything—the wreck of the building, the grass, what was left of the Pentagon's helicopter pad. Few large pieces of the plane were found, testimony to the plane's speed and force as it hit the building.

The massive wall—recently reinforced as part of a long-planned renovation—had collapsed in on itself. Most was indistinguishable wreckage, but oddly, a few items survived unscathed. A desk sat alone in an office whose walls had been sheared off. A clock hung above what had been a door jamb, the door blown away.

Fire continued to burn as we walked quietly around the crash site. Flight 77, a Boeing 757, had left nearby Dulles Airport and was on its way to Los Angeles before the hijackers took over. It was fully loaded with fuel that continued to burn in the wreckage for a few days after 9/11.

As we headed back into the building, we passed uniformed personnel standing quietly over bodies covered in white sheets. Some were on the grass near the crash site, others were placed carefully in the Pentagon's inner courtyard. All 64 people on the plane were killed, as well as 125 people inside the Pentagon. More than a hundred people were seriously injured and had to be taken to nearby hospitals.

I felt it was critical that Rumsfeld do a media briefing that day and that he do it in the Pentagon. Others objected. Smoke and water damage in the building were getting worse. It might be impossible to get the briefing room ready or the press down from the CITGO what with all the security. Regardless, many said, it didn't matter where he did the briefing. I disagreed completely. I was insistent: a briefing in the Pentagon would be the most powerful statement we could deliver that we were open for business. I went up to the secretary.

"We're working on getting you out to brief. Most people think we shouldn't do it in the building. I think it's critical that it be in the Pentagon."

"Why do they object?" Rumsfeld asked. I explained their

logistical concerns and my belief in the symbolic importance of a briefing in the building. Rumsfeld looked me over.

"Can you get it done?"

"Yes, sir."

"Then do it."

At six or six thirty, Rumsfeld, Warner, Levin, and General Shelton—who had arrived from his overseas trip—headed toward the briefing room. A thought hit me as we reached the top of the stairs leading down to the briefing room.

"Gentlemen, you need to remember that *millions and millions and millions* of people around the world will be watching you, and a lot of them are scared. You need to be confident and reassuring. And you need to demonstrate that *nothing* will stop our government from operating."

They nodded. My message wasn't exactly novel, but it was important that we focus on it before the briefing began.

Flashbulbs bathed the room in light as they entered. The mood in the room was somber. The reporters looked exhausted. Rumsfeld walked up to the podium and—in a straightforward, all-business tone—read the statement he had written out by hand.

> This is a tragic day for our country. Our hearts and prayers go to the injured, their families and friends. We have taken a series of measures to prevent further attacks and to determine who is responsible. We're making every effort to take care of the injured and the casualties in the building. I'm deeply grateful for the many volunteers from the defense establishment and from the excellent units from all throughout this region. They have our deep appreciation. We have been working closely throughout the day with President

Bush, Vice President Cheney, CIA Director George Tenet, the vice chairman of the Joint Chiefs of Staff, Dick Myers, who is currently participating in a meeting elsewhere in the building, and a great many other officials from throughout the government. . . . It's an indication that the United States government is functioning in the face of this terrible act against our country. I should add that the briefing here is taking place in the Pentagon. The Pentagon's functioning. It will be in business tomorrow.

Rumsfeld took a handful of questions, refusing—as we had earlier in the day—to speculate about any uncertain information. Afterward, he left for the White House. I returned to my office and started working the phones to check on staff and return calls. Sometime around midnight, I headed home. Crossing the Potomac again, I saw well-armed military policemen lining the bridge. Wow, I reflected. That's something you thought you'd never see. When I got home, I changed out of my clothes, which reeked of smoke, dumped them in the basement, headed upstairs, and checked in on the kids. They were all in one bedroom, sprawled all over each other. They looked so peaceful, a total contrast to what I'd seen the rest of the day.

Exhausted, I woke Brian up to let him know I was home. Neither of us had an ounce of energy to spare.

"You OK?" he mumbled.

"Yeah," I groaned back. "You OK?"

"Yeah."

That was all that mattered right then. I tumbled into bed to catch a couple of hours of sleep.

I have spent more than twenty years in the communications

business, a period that reaches from the long-gone heyday of the daily newspaper to the birth of twenty-four-hour news to the onset of the Internet. Looking back, though, I believe that September 11, 2001, encapsulated every lesson about effective communications I've ever learned.

Our fundamental message—the Pentagon is open for business—was simple and straightforward, and we repeated it literally thousands of times in that day. We began as early in the day as we could, as soon as the press made it to the CITGO. As early as possible we got the top official—Rumsfeld himself—out in front of the cameras. Rather than managing the flow of information, we facilitated it: in the environment of September 11 and the days that followed, the more people knew, even if it was unsettling, the safer they would feel and the better decisions they would make. At the same time, we treated the accuracy of information as a brand standard: under no circumstances, for no reason, would we release any information we couldn't verify.

September 11 illustrated the most fundamental—and fundamentally new—fact of communicating in today's interconnected, hyperconnected world: the age of spin is over, and the age of transparency has begun. But that never occurred to us. We never gamed out who would be blamed for the attacks, hyperanalyzed the best time in the news cycle for a briefing, or scrutinized every piece of information to ask how it would shape the story. We took every bit of accurate information we had and got it out as quickly as we could.

September 11, of course, was an extraordinary day. But from the Keating Five scandal in the late 1980s to the war in Iraq in 2003, I've learned over and over that sunshine trumps spin every time. The implications of that fact are enormous, and I return to that old aphorism: you can put lipstick on a pig, but it's still a pig. If you've got a pig on your hands—which is to say, a tough story—no lipstick can be laid on thick enough to cover up that fact.

Smart communicators acknowledge that fact; smarter ones embrace it. Because once you figure out you can't put lipstick on a pig, what you've really learned is far more powerful: you've learned not to produce a pig in the first place. Smart communicators know they can't talk their way out of dumb decisions, so they know, better than anyone, the paramount importance of getting it right to start with. Organizations—from multinationals to the military—that integrate communications into decision making make smarter decisions.

Even better, when you come up with a prettier product than a pig—no offense, incidentally, to pigs, especially the many who have laid down their lives at our annual pig roasts with apples lodged in their mouths—you can use the very same sunshine to ensure it's appreciated and seen. Sunshine forces you to get it right; it also enables you to show people that you did.

We live in a period of disintermediation. From warehouse-type stores like Price Club to factory outlet malls to direct-to-consumer sales on the Internet, people are disinclined to deal with—and pay—middlemen. Communications is no exception: consumers can now find information direct from the source, without the news media serving as intermediaries. There was a time, for example, when a restaurant could manage its public relations by keeping an eagle eye cocked for the reviewer at the one major daily paper in town. Today, online entertainment sites—many run by those same newspapers—routinely include postings from everyday folks reviewing their latest experience at the restaurant in question. It's bad news for lousy restaurants, and a terrific opportunity for genuinely and consistently good ones. These days, were a chef or restaurant manager to ask a smart communications pro how to manage public relations, the answer would be simple: serve good food.

Perhaps it all seems self-evident. But to many people in the communications business, the triumph of transparency over spin is still counterintuitive. They were trained in applying lipstick to pigs. That, many believe, is where their worth lies. It's the contribution they make, the justification for their salaries, offices, and expense accounts. Most modern strategies for public communications were built on an edifice of spin—the belief that anything could be explained away if only the explainer was sufficiently creative, quick-witted, and conniving. Especially in politics, a whole mythology sprung up around the art of the spin: the master "spin doctor" could, or so the legend went, extract anyone from any problem by trumping substance with style. The media could be charmed, the public distracted, and the story stopped.

If that was ever true—a dubious proposition in itself—it is no more. Spin may survive in the shadows, but it disintegrates in the sunshine. And in the era of the Internet, twenty-four-hour news, and a proliferation of publications precisely tailored to every demographic subset, a blinding light is shining in every corner of public and private life. There is, simply put, nowhere to hide. The volume and velocity of information have rendered spin impossible and irrelevant. As Enron and MCI can attest, institutions built on illusions collapse in real time. Those who interact with the public—and today, that covers just about everyone, from corporate executives and cabinet secretaries in the office to salesmen and soldiers on the front lines—must accept the defining feature of strategic communications in the Information Age: the death of spin.

I say "accept," but the real point is that this phenomenon should be embraced. The death of spin is a good thing—not just for the listening and viewing public, but for communicators too. In the postspin era, decision makers—stripped of the delusion that spin can rescue them from their mistakes—will make better, smarter, more defensible choices. Vast new avenues of communication—many of which connect decision makers with their constituencies directly, one-on-one, without a filter, and therefore without distortion by the media—are spread before them.

Even for public figures facing sticky situations, the death of spin is an opportunity: by shooting straight, they can both survive controversy and enhance their reputations.

In the movie *City Slickers*, the grizzled cowboy Jack Palance advises an anxiety-ridden Billy Crystal: "Do you know what the secret of life is? One thing. Just one thing." That's good advice for persuasive communications too. Here's my version: embrace transparency. In good times or bad, putting a big spotlight on your story will make it better. Revel in the honesty of transparency and appreciate its efficiency.

This book is, in that sense, more than a warning not to put lipstick on a pig. It's about new opportunities for public communications in the Information Age. These days, there's nowhere to hide from the sunshine. Instead, figures in the public eye should bask in it.

ACKNOWLEDGMENTS

Growing up outside Pittsburgh, I never dreamed I would write a book. And every time I nervously checked my contract with Simon & Schuster to reconfirm my obligations, I was surprised to read my name next to the words "the author." How I got here is a long story with a common thread—the amazing people in my life. I have been lucky to work for wonderful bosses at so many of the (many) places I have worked. I'm surrounded by wonderful friends, and I have an incredible family that always says "why not?" instead of "why you?" In that environment, it's easy to do just about anything. And it's easy to be good at communications when you can learn from so many talented people.

My brief attempts at journalism were cut short by Time, Inc. folding the *Washington Star* in 1981, but for over two wonderful years I worked for Gary Hoenig, a creative genius and compassionate leader. From him, I learned the power of images, the benefits of risk taking and—above all—the decency of caring for those who work with you.

For sheer passion, John McCain has few equals. I reveled in that energy for several years and learned that "when in doubt, lean forward," was a good approach to communications.

Only Carla Hills could apply discipline to a field as amorphous as communications, and she did it superbly as the U.S. Trade Representative. From her I gained organizational skills that improve every product, large and small. As important, her devotion to family and friends showed me that you could be in eighteen places at once and have a heck of a lot of fun doing it.

From Decker Anstrom, I learned that if you work hard enough, you can teach pigs to fly. And even when they crash to the ground trying, you can be gracious about it.

Just when you think you know something, you encounter somebody who knows it better. Case in point: Secretary Rumsfeld. His instincts on the "new realities" of the information era were years ahead of others', including mine. His willingness to embrace new strategies to overcome the challenges of the information revolution made my job much easier. His commitment to our country is inspirational, his sense of humor and friendship a treasure I will cherish for a long time. And many thanks to JR (aka Joyce Rumsfeld) for her boundless enthusiasm and compassion, and for taking precious time from her schedule to offer sage counsel on this book.

Any success I had at the Pentagon was due largely to the people with whom I worked at DOD Public Affairs. Chief among them is Army Colonel George H. Rhynedance, my senior military assistant, right hand man, confidante, and true class act. Any mistakes were mine despite his best efforts to save me from myself. George did not seek the job but accepted it graciously and tackled it with ferocious dedication. To say my work at the

Pentagon was easy would be a slight stretch, but George's two hours for every one of mine made my life much better.

Of enormous help to both of us was Major Riccoh Player. Yes, we had a Major Player, and we were so fortunate to have Riccoh. He kept the kittens happy and me sane on many long trips. The harder the challenge, the more Riccoh liked it, and he made the toughest problems look easy.

Among the Navy's finest is Admiral T. McCreary, one of the true outside-the-box communications thinkers. "T"'s commitment to telling the military story—good and bad—motivated many of us and gave us our bearings in turbulent times. Despite many commitments to job and family, "T" took time to help me with this book, suggesting changes that improved its accuracy, content, and delivery.

I was honored to work with Bryan Whitman, one of my deputies, and Air Force Colonel Jay DeFrank. Both gave their work in Public Affairs their best every day, no matter how long the hours or how numerous the tasks. They tackled the many challenges I threw at them with enthusiasm and never made (too much) fun of my difficulties with military jargon. Despite my admiration for Jay, however, I will never forgive him for putting me on the Jon Stewart show.

Larry Di Rita is a friend, trusted adviser, and inspired public servant. Larry always had an open door, a word of support, and a healthy dose of humor to defuse tough situations. From my Senate confirmation process to my last days at the Pentagon, I counted on and benefited from his help every day. Despite a crushing schedule, Larry, too, took the time to read the book, caution against wrong turns I was taking, and offer constructive advice I embraced wholeheartedly.

Anyone who knows Steve Cambone knows that he is often the smartest guy in the room. What many don't know is that he is passionately patriotic, extremely patient, and man enough to eat crow (and carry one down the hallway) when appropriate. The country is lucky to have him working for us, and I am lucky to have him as a friend.

Few people are very nice and very successful, but Bob Barnett is both. Thanks so much to him for making this book happen and for taking such good care of my post–public service life.

Many people agreed to read various early versions of *Lipstick on a Pig,* and I am sure they regretted that decision the second the draft hit their desks. Lisa Boepple reminded me of the difference between the Bahamas and Bermuda and offered encouragement at the very time I was questioning why I ever started the project in the first place. For that and for her friendship over many years I am very grateful. Jamie Sterling will do just about anything for a pal, and I tested the bounds of our friendship by seeking his help on the book. He actually read the whole draft and gave good advice that changed its direction in a meaningful way. Mary Matalin is a friend in good times and bad, and we've had our share of both. I am in her debt for her help and encouragement on the book, of course, but also for her wise advice over the years. (Maybe I can hire your girls some day, Mary.) Peter Hart, true to form, started his critique of the book with the positives and then quickly turned to the important steps that would make it better. When you say, "be honest with me," Peter is, and I am very grateful for his advice on this and many projects.

Lori Voles (Lorraine to those of you who have known her for only the last twenty years) and I have a friendship that stretches back through schools, bars, boyfriends, husbands, and families. For her insightful comments and suggestions on the book—all of which I adopted—I owe her a lifetime of thanks and many glasses of wine at the neighborhood bar.

Barbara Coons did an amazing job of researching, finding the obscure quote, verifying the dates, and correcting many mistakes. Greg Weiner helped lay the book's foundation and tried to teach me how to write. He's a gifted writer and good friend.

Dominick Anfuso and Wylie O'Sullivan of Simon & Schuster shared their skill and experience in the most remarkably patient way, and never laughed at my goofy questions about how to publish a book—at least not to my face.

The fact that I survived writing this book is another example of my parents' patience and support for yet another adventure on my part. Thanks to them for everything, and a special thanks to my father, Charles E. Clarke, who could give up his successful medical practice and go into editing.

To my husband, Brian, and our kids, Colin, Devan, and Charlie, for their encouragement and love, and for not asking more than twice a week, "Aren't you done with that book yet?"

INDEX

ABOUT THE AUTHOR

TORIE CLARKE is a former Pentagon spokeswoman and the former Assistant Secretary of Defense for Public Affairs under Defense Secretary Donald Rumsfeld. She frequently delivered televised press briefings as one of Defense Secretary Rumsfeld's top aides, and made appearances on programs ranging from *60 Minutes* to *Good Morning America* to *The Daily Show* with Jon Stewart. She was also press secretary for President George H. W. Bush's 1992 re-election campaign, and served as Assistant U.S. Trade Representative for Public Affairs and Private Sector Liaison during the first Bush Administration. Prior to that she was a close adviser to Senator John McCain during his early Congressional career. Clarke is currently a senior adviser to Comcast and on air contributor for CNN.

Clarke has advised and lectured before some of the nation's best-known executives. She has served as President of Bozell Eskew advertising, head of the Washington office of the public relations firm of Hill and Knowlton, and Vice President of the National Cable Telecommunications Association.

Clarke lives in suburban Washington with her husband, Brian Graham, and three children, Colin, Devan, and Charlie.